Urban Legends

Urban Legends

Nick Harding

www.pocketessentials.com

This edition published in 2005 by Pocket Essentials
P.O.Box 394, Harpenden, Herts, AL5 1XJ

www.pocketessentials.com

Distributed in the USA by Trafalgar Square Publishing, P.O. Box 257, Howe Hill Road,
North Pomfret, Vermont 05053

A CIP catalogue record for this book is available from the British Library.

ISBN 1 904048 35 8

2 4 6 8 10 9 7 5 3 1

Typeset by Avocet Typeset, Chilton, Aylesbury, Bucks
Printed and bound in Great Britain by Cox & Wyman Ltd, Reading, Berks

For my family

and dedicated to the
memories of

David Hall BA MA Oxon

Poet, Friend…

and

Jackson Newton

Nephew…

ACKNOWLEDGEMENTS

For friends around the globe who have been so supportive throughout the years. They are, of course far too numerous to mention (they know who they are!) but special thanks must be given to Tim Calvert, Sean Martin, Nick Richards, Doctors Jerry Kaye and Fiona Thompson, Andy Stansfield, Mikey B, Helen Harrow and Kesia, Neil Creek, Keith and Zoe, Ian Brindle, The Clan Morton, Doug Elford Argent, Ian S and Adders W, Willo Treschow and Paul, David Anderson, Kate, Emma, Clare, Helen, Sarah, Candy, Toby, Dicky and Pete, Richard Cheek and all in the Bristol Exploration Club. Special mention must be made to Dr Susan Blackmore for her kind assistance with the section on memes and to Nick Rennison for knocking the text into shape.

Contents

"Experto credite"
(Believe one who knows by experience)
Virgil, *Aeneid*

Preface

strange, uneasy, curious

URBAN MYTH *or* LEGEND: *n* A story, esp. one with a shocking or amusing ending related as having actually happened, usu. to someone vaguely connected with the teller.

Collins English Dictionary.

Urban Legends occupy a unique position in human culture. They are a bridge between true story telling, the realm of fantasy, and the real world. They exist on the boundaries where the definitions of what is true and what is imaginary lack solidity and clarity. They are stories that blur the edges. We pride ourselves, particularly in this day and age, on being intelligent, aware and conscious of the world around us. We think that we are less likely, in this modern world of instant information, to fall victim to the scam, dupe or tall story. We do not believe in a flat Earth or that the stars are fixed to crystal spheres. We know that the planets revolve around the sun. We know the age of the universe, the speed of light and the workings of quantum mechanics. But somehow, despite these advances, Urban Legends still hold sway. Why is this so?

Urban Legends have survived so long because

humans tell stories and have done so from the Palaeolithic campfire to the bar in the local pub. The reasons for doing so are numerous. Stories are told as social bonding devices. They can be tools for self-aggrandisement or used for the transmission of information. They can be a means of instruction, particularly in the realm of morality and mores, and, in some cases, they can be used as a device to control the behaviour of others, from groups of small children to whole nations. Even in an electronic age stories are still important to our species. One only has to look at the continuing popularity of TV, film, novels and computer games to realise that the telling of stories is very much alive and will survive as long as there are humans to tell them. Stories are a social glue – we need them, probably more than ever at the start of a new millennium (something that has itself contributed to the creation of Urban Legends), as great swathes of the population around the globe feel, rightly or wrongly, that they are entering a more precarious era. Stories bring security – a shared experience and a communality that helps us all deal with the wider world – but they can also delude us and encourage enormous misconceptions about our society and our position in it.

The most interesting aspect of Urban Legends is that they seem to defy critical destruction. In fact they are thriving more than ever before. After the attacks on the Twin Towers in New York on 11 September 2001 a number of Urban Legends began circulating and were reported at all levels of the media as if they were true. Unsurprisingly, the tabloids ran the stories but the same

Legends were being recounted in the broadsheets and in news broadcasts. The most famous of these was the *Thankful Stranger*, usually a man of Middle Eastern appearance, who, having had his dropped wallet returned, tells the good Samaritan to avoid a certain Tube station (the location varies – a true indicator the story is an Urban Legend) on a certain day at a certain time (these also vary). The durability of Urban Legends rests in their superficial credibility – they could after all be true. Therein lies their strength. There is a sense with all Urban Legends that somewhere, and at sometime, they actually happened as described. They are clever enough to fool all of us, however savvy we think we are.

This book will set out to describe Urban Legends in all their popular forms and will offer some reasons for their durability. It will look particularly at one way of analysing them – through the idea of the 'meme', a self-replicating element of culture. It will highlight the most famous of the stories and discuss legends as cultural symbols and the means by which they permeate every level of human social interaction.

The subject is, of course, vast with new material appearing almost daily and it is therefore recommended that the reader acquaint himself, or herself, with at least www.snopes.com, the website that investigates such tales, and the FOAFTALE NEWS: The Newsletter of the International Society For Contemporary Legend Research.

N.B. *Urban Legends* is the correct nomenclature for these stories – *Urban Myths* is a misnomer. Myths deal with the activities of mythical beings such as gods, goddesses and the like.

Introduction

This book sets out to examine the enduring appeal of those stories (e.g. *The Phantom Hitchhiker, The Beast Of Bodmin, The Dog In the Microwave*) that all of us have heard at sometime, accepted as true and passed on as such to others, delighting in their telling with a certain degree of *schadenfreude*. Scholars and folklorists recognise these oft–quoted tales as a fundamental part of our ongoing story–telling tradition and that they are nothing more than Urban Legends that have developed like Chinese Whispers. These are tales that have grown in the telling but which have no basis in reality.

We have all heard them and we have all accepted them as true, convincing ourselves that somewhere the incidents retold must have actually happened to some poor unsuspecting victim. Our ideas about their authenticity are supported by their retelling in the popular media which has often become a willing participant in their propagation, reporting the incidents as real–life events rather than fiction.

Urban Legends cross into many other areas, taking in UFOs, alien abductions, ghosts and other accounts of the supernatural. It has been argued that 'alien abduction' stories are a modern Urban Legend in the making and, through the all-pervasive power of the media, they have become accepted as the truth by many people. The X-Files, for example, picks up an Urban Legend and turns it into a TV programme. This solidifies the 'falsehood' into 'reality', thus retroactively giving support to the original source material. In a very real sense, Urban Legends become a medium through which important ideas are transmitted from one generation to the next, similar in many respects to fairy tales in which sub–textual meanings are hidden.

Urban Legends work hand in hand with folklore. There may not, in reality, be much difference between them. They are just different sides of the same coin. Urban Legends have much in common with age-old legends and folk tales about hidden treasure, ghosts, Robin Hood and so on. They are told with the same deliberate earnest conviction. They are passed on by word of mouth, are generally anonymous and vary constantly in terms of particular details, often altered by the storyteller who adds his or her own shine to a well polished tale already bright through years of telling. Common to both is a central core of traditional elements and iconic motifs that span generations and are cross–cultural. These fit neatly into the broad range of human experience and readily move across the borders of nations and cultures.

Urban Legends have to be understood as being inherently false, at least in the sense that the extraordinary events could not actually have happened in so many places around the world to so many relatives, friends, and friends of friends of the millions of tellers of the tales. On the other hand what must be taken as true is that the stories themselves tend to be a subconscious (sometimes conscious) reflection of the concerns of the individuals in the societies in which the legends circulate and evolve. For example, the First World War story of The Angel Of Mons (which, despite continuing debate about its authenticity, in fact owed its origin to a newspaper article written by Arthur Machen as a propaganda piece) spread so quickly because it offered hope and meaning amid the chaos and anarchy of the war.

Contemporary stories of bodily invasion by parasites or snakes may, in fact, reflect a fear of society being invaded by outsiders. Recent events such as the World Trade Centre attacks have spawned a new wave of Urban Legends involving individuals heading to the doctors complaining of a stomach ache only to be told that there is a large tropical snake, or other horrific creature, growing inside them. Genuine fears of invasion are thus reflected in the stories told to someone by a friend of a friend of an individual who happened to be listening to a conversation in a coffee house. When a nation is fearful its Urban Legends increase in frequency to reflect that. A classic Urban Legend centred around the World Trade Centre is rooted in the fear of another attack – the mysterious stranger on the subway thanking someone for a good deed done, usually the return of a lost wallet, and then warning them not to be in a particular place at a particular time. A variation of this one even made it to this side of the Atlantic.

Fifty years ago similar fears were being expressed in the 'Reds Under the Beds' scare in the United States. This was reflected in all sorts of cultural and social phenomena, from movie scripts to the House Committee on UnAmerican Activities and the trials which it instigated. This example, in which an Urban Legend becomes a major political issue, is a stark reminder to us that they are not just harmless tales.

Urban Legends also fall into the category of what Professor Richard Dawkins and Dr Susan Blackmore call 'memes' – ideas that are spread almost like viruses within human cultural structures, a concept that is starting to be taken seriously by the scientific community. These memes have a life of their own and replicate themselves rapidly as humans come into contact with each other. They may be as simple as a jingle from a television advert or they may be a more complex network of interconnecting memes (called a 'memeplex') such as a religion.

This book will not debunk Urban Legends but will explain their development and something of their history. It will look at some classic Urban Legends, many of which have inspired enough Hollywood movies to become clichés yet remain effective because they are part of the human subconscious. (*Scream* is an obvious example. It taps into the 'teenage horrors' subset of Urban Legends and teenagers themselves provide one of the most important channels for these tales.) The book will also outline the various 'themes' around which Urban Legends can be grouped. There are many distinct types such as, for example, 'body contamination', 'nudity' or 'teenager in peril'. It will also outline some modern variations including that of 'alien abduction' which operates very much in the realm of the classic fairy story, taking in the fear of outsiders as part of its psychological source and developmental process along the way. As our technology improves exponentially and we learn more about our universe and our place within it, Urban Legends are proving as persistent and powerful as ever. The Internet has provided a new and potent channel for these tales to be transmitted around the world – improving the transmission rate and ensuring their durability.

Part One

Behind the Legends

Themes

Urban Legends are grouped by folklorists into *'Themes'* for easy identification and within each theme *'subtypes'* occur. Subtypes are stories which have a distinct plot of their own but which share basic elements of the larger theme e.g. *Worm Burger* is a subtype of *The Mouse in A Bottle* which is in itself a major example of the *Food Contamination* theme.

Examples of themes include *'Teens In Peril'*, *'Food Contamination'*, *'Body Contamination'*, *'The Horrendous-Discovery'*, *'The Phantom Hitchhiker'* (sometimes known as *'The Vanishing Hitchhiker'*) and *'The Death Car'*.

Tale In The Telling

Urban Legends on the whole (other than *fixed point* stories, see Glossary) tend to have no specific geographical location, but are adapted by the storyteller to reflect his or her environment. A tale told by children around a campfire in Maine will take in areas known to them – places that may already be charged with emotional power e.g. 'The Haunted Mill Yard' or 'The Witch House'. The same Legend may turn up in Greenbay, Minsk or Copenhagen but the storytellers will use locations specific to them which are guaranteed to provoke an immediate response of horror in their eager listeners. The Mill Yard in Maine may become the Ship Yard in Copenhagen or the Canning Factory in Minsk and so on. An emotionally charged location may also act as a 'magnet' for different types of Urban Legends. An abandoned house may have once been the home of a killer involved in the murder of two teenagers who stayed there over night to escape a terrible storm (*Teens in peril*). The same house may have once been the home of a madman who chopped up his victims to sell to a local butchers (*Food Contamination*) or it may have been the location of a body that was found in a car months after a disappearance (*Death Car*).

Whatever the case the story will always have the appearance of being the truth and the location will always be somewhere known and, more often than not, in the immediate vicinity of teller and listener. The endangered protagonists are usually nameless but they are the kinds of people that are recognisable (sometimes stereotypically) to those telling and to those listening to the Legend.

Another important factor in the description of Urban Legends is the *Relative Chain* or the chain along which the tale has apparently travelled. The narrator will always say that they heard the story from a 'friend of a friend' or 'a friend of a cousin of mine' or any number of combinations thereof. This *Relative Chain* is nearly always missing in the media, particularly in newsprint, but will often be present if an interviewee is asked to describe an event.

Despite our world being dominated by mobile phones, the Internet and 24-hour news coverage people still have this desire to talk to each other. Technology has not yet (and it probably never will) replace the comfort gained from face to face contact with another human being. Our basic need to interact and to exchange information on a personal level seems little diminished despite the electronic noise that surrounds us. We still have the desire to tell or listen to stories because they seem to hold basic truths about the world we live in. But, to compete, Urban Legends have had to take on more of the mantle of being factual and have to be presented in a snappy news-style delivery and, like the daily news, they have to be concerned with death, accidents, injuries, misfortune, scandals and tragedies. In fact they are evolving to survive in a modern world.

Origins

One of the great mysteries surrounding Urban Legends concerns their origin points. These stories can be tracked around the world but no single source location can be found for any of them – other than those with a *fixed point* (see Glossary) such as the stories surrounding the Twin Towers. They change, shift and alter their elements in an adaptive process so that no amount of research can pinpoint an exact location or place in time where the Legend first came to life. Leads may be followed but they will always come to a dead end where the original events behind the tale have simply vanished. If, indeed, they ever existed.

Some Legends may begin as nothing more than rumours born from a misinterpretation of phenomena or a half-heard set of circumstances wrongly assessed and passed on as a factual event or series of events. Some rumours may in fact blend together. They start out as totally unconnected but through the story-telling process and the narrator's willingness to entertain and improve the material, a proto–Urban Legend springs into being, one that evolves as it is spread.

When Kenneth Arnold saw strange flying objects

over Mount Rainer in 1947, he described them as moving as a saucer would, skipping over water. Nowhere does he say they were 'flying saucers'. But the word 'saucer' was seized upon and spread by the media. The testing of secret aircraft and of captured German technology after World War 2 was seen by casual, uninformed witnesses and contributed grist to the mill of the rumour-mongers. From a third direction came the misinterpretation of natural celestial occurrences. Together these drove that particular Legend on, the elements all now mingling to form a whole that has become the 'UFO myth'.

Folklore and Urban Legends

Urban Legends form a distinct subclass of folklore. They are stories that, unlike fairy tales, are believed to be true or at the very least seem believable because they contain elements that support the notion that they are factual. In the Legend of *The Beast of Bodmin*, for example, the idea that big cats may have escaped and are wandering the countryside is not beyond the bounds of credibility.

Whereas myths are set in a 'distant past' and involve the activities of gods, goddesses and other supernatural beings from angels to Minotaurs, Urban Legends are set in the recent past and have normal people, in everyday, often banal, environments as their protagonists. They are quasi-folk history gaining their credibility from the use of real places, known products and other modern elements that are easily recognisable and to which importance and therefore a high level of believability can be attached. Put crudely, we know there are teenagers, that there are cars and that there are places where teenagers gather to make out. Therefore it is not beyond the bounds of credibility to suggest that someone with murderous leanings is watching their activities and that the teenagers themselves may fall victim to him. That this individual sports a hook or some other unusual weapon is the *pivot point* (see Glossary) of this particular Urban Legend.

As Jan Harold Brunvand has written, 'Folklore subsists on oral tradition but not all oral communication is folklore'. Most human communication including jokes, business meetings, gossip, teaching and so on rarely becomes folklore but more often than not these 'communicative events' contain elements of traditional material that are memorable (often subconsciously) and easily repeatable. Thus, on one level at least, folklore persists and evolves, hidden within our jokes, proverbs, wisecracks and anecdotes and other 'conversational genres'.

Some folklore forms, such as fairy tales, myths, songs etc. may continue only in certain circumstances and may only develop in distinct social groups dependent entirely on 'oral dissemination', containing internal patterns and recurring motifs and themes without which the stories would wither and die. These internal structures allow the folk tale to survive while the external variations, that allow the story to be replicated, alter, shift and vary as the story is retold. Urban Legends behave, in many ways, like evolution with the story adapting to its environment so that it may survive.

In contrast to this is the idea of the *fixed location*. The Legends surrounding the destruction of the Twin Towers have a fixed point from which they originate. Urban Legends sourced from that tragedy will not survive by adaptation to, say, Canary Wharf. We know that nothing like that has happened in London and that

Canary Wharf still stands. Whereas an Urban Legend like the *Poodle In The Microwave* is so generic it has greater survivability – it can transfer to any restaurant in any city anywhere in the world. Of course the opposite is true. Some extant Urban Legends can be adapted to suit the paranoia surrounding the Twin Towers. For example, *Body Contamination* stories may increase as a direct result of greater fear and paranoia born from that incident. A fear of the outsider – 'the terrorist' – is already a deep-rooted psychological condition in present day United States.

To understand folklore and therefore the realm of the Urban Legend is to understand the psyche of a nation.

Tall Stories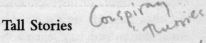

Storytelling is an inherent part of human existence and has been with us for as long as humans have been able to speak. It is one form of social cohesion or a process of bonding. Everyone tells stories in their workplace, school, home or at any number of social gatherings. It is an important part of our lives. It fuels our entertainment industries and educates us in moral, religious and social behaviour.

Stories themselves come in three distinct types. 1) ACTUAL – stories which recount actual events such as holidays, narrow scrapes in accidents, a blossoming or failing romance. 2) CREATED – the invented stories of novels, films, comic books etc. 3) LEGENDS AND MYTHS. Though these two latter terms are often used interchangeably and, more often than not, confused, they have separate and specific meanings. Both myths and legends contain casts of characters and plotlines followed to their conclusions and yet their core elements are different. Myths are tales about the acts of godlike or supernatural beings and/or magical animals which serve to explain the creation of the world or how certain elements of our world came to be and they take place in the far reaches of time. (Often they begin with phrases like, 'In the days when the world was new'). By contrast, legends are accounts of purported incidents involving ordinary people in more recent times. Although both types of stories are told as true, they are not necessarily believed to be literal truth by either the tellers or their audiences.

Urban Legends are a specific class of legend, differentiated from 'ordinary' legends by their being provided as, and being believed to be, accounts of actual incidents that befell or were witnessed by someone the teller almost knows (e.g., his sister's best friend's hairdresser's plumber). These tales are told as true, local, and as recent occurrences and often contain names of places within the teller's neighbourhood or surrounding region, that will evolve, adapt and change depending on the storyteller, to give additional spice to the tale.

Urban Legends are narratives, which put our fears and concerns into the form of stories, which we use to confirm and indeed reinforce the 'rightness' of our worldview, biased as that may be. As cautionary tales they warn us against engaging in risky behaviours by pointing out what has supposedly happened to others who did what we might be tempted to try. Other legends confirm our suspicions that it's a dangerous world out there, one awash with crazed killers, lurking terrorists, unscrupulous companies out to make a buck at any cost and governments that care little for their citizens. Reinforcement for these stories comes in the guise of very real news events where people are indeed kidnapped by killers (recent events in Australia) where members of the public are assaulted in their cars (numerous road rage incidents) or where young children die at the hands of paedophiles (The Soham murders).

True or False?

On the whole we commonly equate an 'Urban Legend' with 'falsehood', particularly when we hear the more famous stories such as *The Phantom Hitchhiker* or *The Nude Surprise Party*. But others elude our critical abilities and, for a long while, remain in the public domain, being told and retold as a truth. An example of this would be the *Challenger Disaster Tapes* Legend in which the story goes that Mission Control in Houston had a tape recording of the last few moments of the astronauts' lives as Challenger plummeted to destruction in the Atlantic Ocean – an Urban Legend born from the reality of the 'Black Box' recorder. This is a prime example of an Urban Legend that sounds convincing. We know that Black Box recorders exist so therefore NASA must have a tape recording of the astronauts. (Incidentally another mistaken belief is that black boxes are indeed black. They are not. They are orange.)

What adds weight to this Urban Legend is that the world saw the disaster unfold on television. No quiet country lane was involved nor was it a friend of a friend of a friend who saw the Shuttle explode. Gravitas is added to the legend because it has sprung from an actual event – a *fixed point*.

Here is the story, as reported in 1994 and collected from the Internet.

A secret NASA tape reveals that the crew of the shuttle Challenger not only survived the explosion that ripped the vessel apart; they screamed, cried, cursed and prayed for three hellish minutes before they slammed into the Atlantic and perished on 28 January 1986.

The tape is said to begin with a startled crewman screaming, 'What happened? What happened? Oh God – No!' Screams and curses are heard. Several crewmen begin to weep and then others bid their families farewell.

Two minutes forty-five seconds later the tape ends. That's when the shuttles crew compartment, which remained intact after the vessel exploded over the Atlantic, hit the ocean at over 2,000 miles per hour, instantly killing the crew.

'Cover up? Of course there was a cover-up,' declared Robert Hotz, a member of the Presidential commission that investigated the disaster. 'NASA can't face the fact that they put these astronauts in a situation where they didn't have adequate equipment to survive. NASA doesn't give a damn about anything but covering its ass,' he said.

The official account released by NASA ends with shuttle pilot Michael Smith saying, 'Uh-oh!' Some NASA employees have evidently heard more – much more. And they provided the rest of the account based on what they've discussed within

NASA in the last five years. The astronauts had time and realized something was happening after the shuttle broke up.

'All shuttle astronauts carry personal recorders and the tape in question apparently came from Christa's (McAuliffe), which was recovered after the shuttle disaster,' said Hotz. Jarvis was sitting beside her, and when he figured out what was happening he said, 'Give me your hand.'

'NASA insists there's nothing like that on tape but they're talking about the mission tape, not Christa's. So they're not lying, but they're not telling the truth, either.'

A journalist with close ties to NASA was even more emphatic. 'There are persistent rumors, dating back to the disaster, that this tape is absolutely bone-chilling.'

The following transcript begins two seconds after NASA's official version ends, with pilot Michael Smith saying, 'Uh-oh!' Times from the moment of takeoff are shown in minutes and seconds and are approximate.

The sex of the speaker is indicated by M or F. "T+" indicates time after lift off.

T+1:15	(M)	What happened? What happened? Oh God, no - no!
T+1:17	(F)	Oh dear God.
T+1:18	(M)	Turn on your air pack! Turn on your air . . .
T+1:20	(M)	Can't breathe . . . choking . . .
T+1:21	(M)	Lift up your visor!

T+1:22	(M/F)	(Screams.) It's hot. (Sobs.) I can't. Don't tell me . . . God! Do it . . . now . . .
T+1:24	(M)	I told them . . . I told them . . . Dammit! Resnik don't . . .
T+1:27	(M)	Take it easy! Move (unintelligible) . . .
T+1:28	(F)	Don't let me die like this. Not now. Not here . . .
T+1:31	(M)	Your arm . . . no . . . I (extended garble, static)
T+1:36	(F)	I'm . . . passing . . . out . . .
T+1:37	(M)	We're not dead yet.
T+1:40	(M)	If you ever wanted (unintelligible) me a miracle . . . (unintelligible) . . . (screams)
T+1:41	(M)	She's . . . she's . . . (garble) . . . damn!
T+1:50	(M)	Can't breathe . . .
T+1:51	(M/F)	(screams) Jesus Christ! No!
T+1:54	(M)	She's out.
T+1:55	(M)	Lucky . . . (unintelligible).
T+1:56	(M)	God. The water . . . we're dead! (screams)
T+2:00	(F)	Goodbye (sobs) . . . I love you, I love you . . .
T+2:03	(M)	Loosen up . . . loosen up . . .
T+2:07	(M)	It'll just be like a ditch landing . . .
T+2:09	(M)	That's right, think positive.
T+2:11	(M)	Ditch procedure . . .
T+2:14	(M)	No way!
T+2:17	(M)	Give me your hand . . .

T+2:19	(M)	You awake in there? I . . . I . . .
T+2:29	(M)	Our Father . . . (unintelligible) . . .
T+2:42	(M)	hallowed be Thy name . . . (unintelligible).
T+2:57	(M)	You . . . over there?
T+2:58	(M)	The Lord is my shepherd, I shall . . . not want. He maketh me to lie down in green pastures . . . though I walk through the valley of the shadow of death, I will fear no evil . . . I will dwell in the house . . .

T+3:15 to end. Static, silence.

The emotional content of the tape helps guarantee this particular legend's survival whatever anyone at NASA might have said or still says by way of a denial. There is a nagging sense that there could, in fact, be tape somewhere and that the words transcribed above were the actual ones spoken by the astronauts moments before their deaths. An unwillingness to dismiss something so charged with emotion means that scepticism takes a back seat, thus enabling this particular legend, and many others like it, to survive. In fact the transmitter of the tale may add a caveat in the telling. 'I have my doubts', they may say, 'but NASA apparently have this tape…' Yet even that feeling of doubt adds a certain something to the process and is in no way a guarantee that anyone else will harbour the same sense of scepticism about the veracity of the story. If it is a good tale then it will be retold and it will possess its own dynamic despite the doubts expressed.

With certain Urban Legends, it must also be taken into consideration that authoritative denial is an almost certain way of having a story spread like wild fire. 'It is denied, therefore it is true,' is often the illogical outcome of this mode of uncritical thinking. Take, for example, Area 51 or Dreamland where it is claimed that captured flying saucers are being back-engineered and flown by US government personnel. In reality nothing more than the testing of top-secret aircraft happens there but if an inquisitive someone asks the question, 'Are there flying saucers at Area 51?', then the inevitable answer will be a categorical 'No'. Perversely, that will be seen as a denial to hide the truth. The Urban Legend takes hold and begins to spread. The fact that the US Government denied Area 51 existed until recently just accelerated the misleading information which prompted many UFO enthusiasts to make erroneous connections and false assumptions. There must be captured alien technology hidden there because the Government denies the place exists and so on.

Urban Legends and Conspiracy Theories

Any divisions between Urban Legends and Conspiracy Theories soon dissolve. The two are sometimes indivisible. They feed off each other and blur their mutual boundaries. One may grow to resemble the other. For example, here's a *conspiracy theory* about WW2 and its causes:

THE U.S. STARTED WW2

It is known that President Bush's family helped to bankroll the Nazis – this was a deliberate ploy to destabilise Europe and in particular Britain's Empire which, although in decline, was the dominant force in world power. A world war with its roots in central Europe would cripple the continent allowing the US to move in and dominate it. Not only that, by securing victory in the Far East the US would control that region of the world as well. Remember the US had suffered an economic crisis in the Wall Street crash and the Great Depression and, as the famous saying has it, 'war is good for business'. America has become the dominant force in world politics – therefore the US started WW2 to control the world economically.

This is, to some extent, a well-reasoned argument. It is, of course, wrong yet it contains within it numerous facts that the reader knows to be true. The creator of the conspiracy theory has drawn on certain undeniable facts and a few Urban Legends and has pulled them together into a paragraph that reads as if it is fact. This Legend/Conspiracy theory is then passed on via numerous channels and filters out into the wide world where it is assimilated. From that point on it may grow with each telling – more and more 'facts' being added to the mix until it reaches a point where it may become an accepted view of world politics and even one day may be mistaken for real history.

Adding facts into the mix does not always make an Urban Legend durable – far from it. It can help, certainly, as the above example proves, but some of the classic Urban Legends have survived through being totally false - the magic ingredient is always that they 'might just be true'. The same applies to conspiracy theories. There is an element of doubt that creeps into the most sceptical of minds with tales such as these, particularly if real facts are woven into the textual tapestry. As with the above example and the one about Area 51, numerous Legends can be drawn together to form a grand conspiracy theory.

Urban Legends and conspiracy theories operate and develop in a similar way. At their core there may be a certain degree of truth and, in their retelling, they become distorted (often by the narrator) to embellish the tale and make it sound more exciting. Conspiracy theories, though, lack a moral subtext and are largely without the social taboo elements that are an important part of the Urban Legend idiom.

Real Events?

Another Urban Legend that has been circulating for a number of years is the *Dead Office Worker*. In this tale a man is seen slumped at his desk in his office apparently asleep when fellow staff turn up for work in the morning. They naturally assume that he has worked through the night and is just catching up on some sleep and he is left alone. This happens for a whole week until someone actually steps into his office to wake him only to discover that the man has been dead for some time. This was reported, as fact, in numerous newspapers on both sides of the Atlantic as late as spring 2004.

Though the vast majority of such tales are pure invention, a handful do turn out to be based on real incidents, and whether or not something actually happened has no bearing on its status as an Urban Legend. What lifts true tales of this type out of the world of news and into the genre of contemporary lore is the blurring of details and the multiplicity of claims that the events happened locally, alterations which take place as the stories are passed through countless hands. Though there might indeed have been an original actual event, it clearly did not happen to as many people or in as many places as the various reiterations of it would have us believe. What singles these stories out as Urban Legends is their ever–changing locations and participants.

One of the classic Urban Legends is *The Mouse in the Coke Bottle,* a variation of the *Food Contamination* type. This is one of the best-known tales of all time and it has variants such as *Worm Burgers* and *Deep Fried Rat*. The University of Minnesota sociologist Gary Fine (*Omni* Magazine January 1980), investigating the truth behind Urban Legends, discovered in appeals-court records that, in fact, dead mice *had* turned up in Coke bottles as well as in soda bottles of other brands. He has documented, between the years 1914 and 1976, 45 cases of 'dead mice found in bottles' which went through the courts. Most of those cases were levelled against Coca Cola, mainly because sales of that brand were so widespread. So one must conclude that at least a few Urban Legends are based on fact. But, as Gary Fine points out, one can dismiss the 'worm burger' variation as false since a pound of worms would actually be more expensive than a pound of ground beef. This simple point has not hindered the propagation of that particular Legend. As for the *Deep Fried Rat*, as with so many Urban Legends, no amount of denial or ridicule or rational explanation will make that particular story disappear.

In fact Urban Legends tend to have a cyclical nature. For example *Teens In Peril* legends were prolific in the 1960s, in all likelihood as a reaction to the much-feared liberal attitudes of the time. During the 1970s and 1980s they subsided only to re-emerge again in the 1990s because the core elements of that subset of legends were used in popular horror movies aimed at the youth market – *Scream, I Know What You Did Last Summer* and their subsequent sequels being the most famous examples. In *Scream*, for example, the opening scene is a complete Urban Legend in itself – *The Killer*

In The House, a classic of the *Teens in Peril* genre. Just as in the 1960s the story reflected fears of teenage permissiveness the resurgence was in direct response to 1980s ideology, perceived loose morality and growing fears surrounding AIDS. In many ways the 'movie killers' themselves were more frightening second time around because the real world threats were themselves far more terrifying. A kind of reciprocity existed between these real world threats and those on screen, each echoing and boosting the other.

Cultural Meaning

Legends need three basic elements if they are to survive. They are: 1) a strong basic story appeal 2) a foundation in actual belief and 3) a meaningful message, usually connected to a moral issue or a cultural fear. *The Mouse in The Bottle* and others with that theme, it can be argued, represent a fear of large heartless companies riding roughshod through society; an irrational fear that impersonal corporations are taking over, changing society and doing anything for a quick profit. In fact, fear and alienation are a major motivating force for Urban Legends and, in most, their inherent gruesomeness acts as a warning to all who may transgress. They are also three act plays, a structure familiar to screenwriters (many of whom, of late, have plundered Urban Legends for script ideas). There is the set-up, the conflict and the pay-off – usually as a twist ending with shock value. Indeed this is another reason why Urban Legends are so successful. They fit into the natural rhythms found in all story structures.

A strong basic story appeal is clear when we consider the nature of the stories told. Urban Legends are awash with killers, threats of invasion, fear, shocking taboo-breaking behaviour and a world almost out of control.

They play on primal human fears, fears that inhabit every level of culture. Fears that hark back to primitive times and ones that are still hot-wired within the human brain. In the retelling of some Urban Legends the role of certain characters may fluctuate from a minor position to that of a major player. For example a policeman coming to the rescue of a stricken young woman (*The Boyfriend's Death*) may originally have been almost non-existent as a character but when a society feels that things are out of control, that anarchy cannot be far away, the role of the policeman increases to one of a saviour – a guiding figure from which the listeners can gain some moral, ethical or judicial comfort.

A foundation in belief is a less tangible part of the Urban Legend because belief is such an arbitrary and indeed a personal thing. For one the existence of a god or gods is taken as an absolute belief – or rather an unswerving truth. To an atheist the notion of a myth-ical unseen being guiding a life is nothing short of nonsense. During the storytelling process there must be a willing suspension of disbelief or a desire to take the story as fact. This is assisted by the art of the storyteller who may seed the story with known places and char-acters to give it an authentic flavour. But, as we have seen, this is not to say that all Urban Legends hold no truth whatsoever. In fact the opposite is true.

In Urban Legends the underlying messages are often very clear and always straightforward, acting in many cases as an explicit warning for the listeners to behave. There is often a sense of poetic justice in the story –

someone behaving foolishly reaps what he or she has sown. Just as fairy tales are rich in subtext (e.g. 'do not stray from the path in the dark wood' acts as a metaphorical injunction to keep one's morals or one's virginity intact) so Urban Legends act as a moral guide or yardstick. There is a sense in many stories that, if you stray from the path, the killer will get you. A sexual subtext more often than not exists. In horror movies aimed at the teenage market, which draw on the themes of Urban Legends, the young maiden who keeps her virginity and behaves in a morally upright way is the one who survives. Anyone else with a freer sexual morality ends up dead.

On a more obvious level stories such as *The Boyfriend's Death* or *The Hook* warn teenagers to stay away from situations in which they may find themselves in danger or, at the very least, to limit their activities within defined parental boundaries. On a larger symbolic scale, in a cultural context, the stories reflect a society's fears about women and the young being left, vulnerable and alone, in a bleak world beyond the safety of the family unit. A direct evolutionary strand in story–telling leads us from primitive societies where to stray beyond the safety of the cave and camp fire meant certain death. The sources of some of the main Urban Legend themes may go back this far. These stories may even reach to the genetic level where a parent will fight to protect its young – an inbuilt instinct in nearly all animals.

Of course a culture must be ripe for infection by an Urban Legend. Stories of phantom hitchhikers will have no place nor will they survive in a society that has no widespread car use but this does not necessarily mean that the Urban Legend of *The Phantom Hitchhiker* will wither and fade. What is more likely to happen is that the story will be dramatically adapted for the indigenous culture. The Kalahari Bushmen are unlikely to recount a story of picking up a hitchhiker in a car but the story they tell will involve perhaps a lone hunter out tracking prey who comes across another lone hunter who joins him in the pursuit until dramatically disappearing at some point in the journey. The startled lone hunter may find himself in a neighbouring village where he learns that the man he describes died the year before. The basic spine of the story is the same as that told in the US or the UK but it has adapted itself to suit the Kalahari. A subliminal and primeval fear of the bush, or the dark beyond the cave is being expressed here.

For any Urban Legend to survive in a culture it must fulfil a need, whether subconsciously or directly. In a generally prosaic world that may be no more than a need to escape reality. Urban Legends can also act as a device for teaching morality, as a warning of the perils of the world or as a way of explaining the unknown. Urban Legends also provide a cultural 'escape' through which bizarre, embarrassing and dangerous situations can be understood. They appeal to the morbid human curiosity for the sensational, much like travelling freak shows once did, and cater for our growing demand for more and more sensational items of news, gossip and chit chat. The more alarming the tale, the better. Today the media is obsessed with the cult of celebrity and that has been a breeding ground for some of the more famous Urban Legends of recent years. The hackneyed tale of a film star and a bizarre sexual practice involving a rodent is a prime example. This Legend thrives because it is based on jealousy of someone else's success but it also works because it brings the celebrity back down to earth, revealing the crude reality beneath the sheen and gloss of Hollywood. In this sense Urban Legends can act as a social leveller – a way of letting off steam about the inconsistencies and hypocrisies of the apparently glamorous. The stories we tell about celebrities allow us to feel normal and to exercise some degree of control in a world where real influence is beyond our reach.

Story Telling

The origins and primary sources of Urban Legends may be unknown but there is no doubt about their modes of replication. These stories exist as a global phenomenon moving through cultures in the same way that songs, fairy tales and myths have done so for millennia but now they have the additional conduits of 24 hour television and the Internet, through which they can move instantaneously around the globe with the click of a few buttons or icons on a screen. What has not changed is the human need to tell stories, the very human desire to gossip and chat to our fellow club members, office workers, passengers, schoolmates, team members and so on. Wherever we congregate stories are told. But story-telling is an art and the well-practised or lively delivery of a story, one that holds the attention of the listeners, may ensure that it survives or develops more than a tale that is given less 'dramatic emphasis'. Is this solely because of the truth content or entertainment value of an individual story or is there something else at work?

Memes

> **"meme** (mi:m), *n. Biol.* (shortened from *mimeme*
> . . . that which is imitated, after GENE *n.*) "An
> element of a culture that may be considered to be
> passed on by non-genetic means, esp. imitation".
> *O.E.D.*

Why do Urban Legends possess a durable survivability?
Why, despite our growing understanding of the world
in a more enlightened age, do these stories continue to
be told and passed on? One theory involves the idea of
'memes'.

In 1976 Professor Richard Dawkins introduced the
idea of memes in his seminal work *The Selfish Gene.* In
this he describes memes as being a vector for the
transfer of ideas throughout culture – anything from a
tune, a catchphrase to an acquired habit or the correct
way to build an arch. This simple but effective concept
was taken up and developed further by Dr Susan
Blackmore in her important book *The Meme Machine.*
Of course the idea of memes is controversial and, like
any new theory, it has both supporters and denouncers
but it is one that is rapidly gaining acceptance. Memes,
under the umbrella term 'memetics', can offer us new

theories about human evolution taking in altruistic behaviour, the development of consciousness and language along the way. Memes may in fact affect us at the genetic level, an exciting enough concept in itself.

But what are memes and how do they relate to Urban Legends? In short, a meme is 'a self replicating element of culture, passed on by imitation'.

Memes, in many respects, behave in a not dissimilar way to genes, as both are replicators. Variation and selection occur when the material is copied or passed on. This is true of Urban Legends. Adaptations, details, place, even the characters may alter on each replication, in other words each telling of the story, but the basic heart of the narrative remains the same. In *The Phantom Hitchhiker* the country the story takes place in may change from the US to the UK, the sex of the hitch-hiker switch from female to male and back to female, and it may be someone's daughter, niece or grandchild yet the basic storyline remains exactly the same. A hitchhiker is picked up on a lonely road and then mysteriously disappears. The good Samaritan later discovers that the person to whom they gave a lift has, in fact, been dead for two, five or ten years. The story evolves, mutates and adapts itself to the society in which it exists and survives by taking on specific cultural references to enable it to replicate further.

In other words an Urban Legend is a meme.

As memes are transferred they lose information and pick up new data, which can lead ultimately to changes in human culture. Sometimes memes occur in large groups or congregate together and are passed on en masse. These are called 'co-adapted meme complexes', or 'memeplexes', for short. Organised religions are the best example of this. In religions a whole panoply of memes (rules, regulations and credos) are passed on. One only has to study the world's religions to see that even there, memes are at work changing their basic tenets or creating schisms within these belief systems. If memes were not at work there would not exist so many variations on a theme. How many versions of Christianity exist in the world today, each claiming to be the best path to the truth?

Ideas like good and evil are also memes. In the real world there is no independent force at work called 'good' nor is there one called 'evil'. These are notions that have somehow survived to the point where most of us cannot look at the world without defining something as good or evil, seeing it in terms of black and white and not shades of grey. Of course these kinds of memes can be useful as a social control. Religions, which Dawkins calls 'viruses of the mind', use the false ideas of good and evil as a way to propagate their meme material. Adherents pass on what they have learnt to others as a method to ensure its survival. Religious organisations also use missionaries, a very obvious meme vector. The memeplex stored in their brains – the belief system – is transferred directly into other cultures using a meme machine – in this case the Missionary.

In one sense all memes can be termed viruses of the mind and they can be just as contagious as their biological counterparts. They are spread almost subliminally from person to person or group-to-group and disseminated throughout society by social interaction, verbal communication and through the media. In this way memes, both large scale and small scale, can be replicated and spread on a global level. With the development and increasing proliferation of the World Wide Web and the Internet, memes can be injected into mass culture at the speed of light and with almost instantaneous television transmission stories, often mistaken as truth, can be beamed from country to country almost as fast. More often than not we are entirely unaware that we are watching and absorbing memes, busy replicating themselves within the constant stream of information that pours from computer screens or television sets into our brains where they are stored to await their inevitable adaptation and eventual transference.

Prior to the global communications revolution memes would have taken a long time to proliferate and would have developed within a limited and confined space, focused, for example, on one tribe or a loose affiliation of tribes, sharing perhaps limited contact until an invading nation brought its own ideas, its modes of dress and (more often than not) its all-powerful religion to bear on the indigenous people. New ways of thinking, of correct attitude and behaviour would have been injected, both consciously and subconsciously, into the society of the conquered. Smoothing the transition from the old ways to the new, these would have largely benefited the conquerors but all would not have been one-way traffic. There would have been some degree of reciprocation. Meme transfer would have worked both ways.

Memes operate both on a basic level (e.g. a craze for yo-yos that sweeps through a school) and on the large scale in the shape of a religion or a recognisable Urban Legend. Many businesses and companies rely on memes to spread their messages to society at large. Adverts use memes in the form of catchphrases or jingles. These enter the mind and take root and a day, a week, maybe years later we find ourselves humming a tune from a commercial. Music itself is a widespread propagator of memes – memes that consist of styles of music, chord sequences, flourishes and so on. Some years ago the meme of 'sampling' started and, at one point, every song that made the charts seemed to have some form of copied sound within its structure. Musicians pick up meme styles and pass them on – much of the Brit Pop revival of the early and mid-1990s, for example, contained references and signatures reminiscent of music of the 1960s.

Memes may also be passed on as types of behaviour. Richard Dawkins describes tutoring a young woman who adopted an unusual response to a question set to her. If the answer required serious thought she would close her eyes tightly, drop her head to her chest and then freeze for half a minute or so while she pondered the question. She would then look up and offer a fluent and intelligent answer. When Dawkins imitated this to a colleague the response was, 'That's Wittgenstein!'. Dawkins discovered that this pupil was the daughter of admirers of the philosopher from whom they had picked up this affectation and subconsciously transmitted it to her. Now this book has picked up the baton and become a transmitting device for that behavioural meme as well, shifting from a behaviour vector to one of the written word, a clear case of memes adapting to survive. It would be interesting to find out, as Dawkins asked, where Wittgenstein picked up that meme.

Some memes become well known and use all kinds of methods of transmission. Today the mass media offer the perfect growing medium for memes. A certain degree of social acceptance is attached to a particular design or name – especially one that has been around for a long time. For example, take Nike who use the name of an ancient Greek winged goddess for victory, together with their famous 'tick' symbol as their logo. The name itself has been part of the collective subconscious for thousands of years and had a meaningful life before its resurgence as a brand name. More people today, of course, know the new meaning rather than the original source but this is a clear example of a meme hijacking an extant name to continue its existence. Memes evolve, change shape and adapt to allow their continued existence. The process is akin to the evolutionary idea of survival of the fittest. Only the strong memes will survive.

Urban Legends evolve as well and, indeed, the strong ones do survive. They adapt and grow with each telling and have a life of their own. As the psychologist Sir Frederic Bartlett said, the storyteller embellishes every tale told with details forgotten or added and the whole iteration and passing on of the tale becomes one large game of Chinese Whispers.

Memes act like living organisms but to say that memes are biological is to suggest the possibility that they can be extracted and dissected under a microscope. They cannot nor can they be measured or quantified. However they do use a biological medium in which to proliferate (human beings) so they should, in some sense, be regarded as living structures not just metaphorically but literally.

Certainly memes are everywhere and a great deal of culture thrives on them but we are not unwilling participants in their survival. They infect our minds but we are not just passive robots passing on memes. As Dr Blackmore says, they are tools with which we think but not everything we think about is a meme. The American philosopher Daniel Dennett argues that our minds and selves are created by an interplay of memes that are constantly shifting and changing – new ones accepted, old ones rejected.

Perhaps there is something of a symbiotic nature to them. When we try to fit in with particular groups we adopt the fashion, mannerisms and ways of speaking common to that human subset. We imitate but we do this to fit in, to be accepted and to feel wanted. Perhaps our own survival is at stake in a kind of mutual gene–meme symbiosis where one helps the other. A loner will soon find his or her genes going extinct so belonging to a group of a mutual status allows greater possibility for the gene's survival. Memes need genes to continue as well. In groups we tell stories to each other in a kind of bonding process. At a party the guests stand around in groups discussing each other's lives and retelling stories they have heard (in some cases these stories turn out to be Urban Legends). But other memes are exchanged here including body language, vocal intonations and delivery, jokes, even fashion.

Most memes are benign but some are destructive. Stereotypical notions – the caricature of the 'mad scientist', to take one example – are passed on as memes even when they are, in the long term, bad for all of us. If there is nothing beneficial in the survival of a *stereotype meme*, how do they manage to continue and thrive?

Various memes (for example scientific thought and theories, literature or art) succeed because they are genuinely useful to us and behave in a benign way. In contrast, other more malign memes use a variety of tricks and manipulations to get themselves copied regardless of whether the information is beneficial to us or not. In short they have to survive. They must replicate and to them that is all that matters. The data they carry does not. This latter group are often called 'selfish memes', a reference to Dawkins's idea of the 'selfish gene'.

Some memes may be in conflict with one another in order to survive. Take for example the iconic image of the Swastika. Before the rise of Hitler and the Nazi party the Swastika or Fylfot was a symbol of good luck or the sun. During World War II the Swastika's meaning was linked to great acts of barbarism and to most of the Western world it continues to be a 'symbol of evil'. But in Buddhist countries, particularly Tibet, the Swastika symbol is still a positive one. In this case there is no doubt which version of the meme is more powerful but there may come a time when the Swastika meme in the West, its survival under threat, will have to adapt and evolve to continue and it will revert back to its original meaning.

There is no doubt that URBAN LEGENDS, as they are passed on, evolve and adapt to their cultural environment but the basic heart of the myth remains the same and, despite regional and national variations, so do the principal elements that go to make up its fabric. What changes within any Urban Legend are the elements that allow it to be transmitted and thus to survive. To all intents and purposes Urban Legends behave like memes.

Interpretation

In interpreting Urban Legends we face the major problem of the lack of substantial information other than who is telling the story, the *relative chain*, and the basic elements of the tale being told. With a news item the location of the incident can be identified and witnesses can be interviewed. With Urban Legends there are no such resources to hand.

Interpretation, then, must rely on the spine of the Urban Legend – the basic story. Elements come and go, are developed and adapted for the indigenous culture in which they thrive and can only be interpreted in terms of the prevailing circumstances of the society in which they exist. The role of certain, usually secondary characters and elements in the stories fluctuates. These secondary elements demand interpretation, since, as Jan

Harold Brunvand writes, 'Folklorists assume that no cultural data is devoid of meaning, and that any data from a culture may cast some light on the meaning of other data from the same culture'. By that he means folklorists should also be willing to draw on a wide range of cultural references when considering an interpretation of an Urban Legend. The stories mirror a society and to refuse to consider certain aspects of that society is to risk coming to false conclusions about their subtext. All corners of a culture from schools and churches to law courts and the media must be examined in search of a Legend's meaning. All kinds of questions need to be asked. To what behavioural norms do the characters in Urban Legends aspire? Which do they disregard? Do they conform or rebel? Is the basic story one of antagonism towards the demands of society or compliance?

Interpretation must involve seeking out the basic *theme* the Urban Legend possesses – a quest for the underlying motif (often a violation of a taboo) that exists at the core of the tale before the real work of overall meaning can be deduced. By comparing these motifs one can assess the historical and psychological connections between cultures. Ultimately, of course, they can be reduced to the quintessential behavioural patterns that are universal to all human societies.

Summary

Urban Legends have a moral subtext

Urban Legends often deal with social taboos

Urban Legends are basically false

Urban Legends evolve and adapt for the surrounding culture

Urban Legends reflect the fears of the society at large

Urban Legends with simple storylines travel further

Urban Legends sometimes have a truthful element at their core

Urban Legends escape the lens of critical scepticism

Urban Legends sometimes fulfil a cultural need

Urban Legends offer a sense of control in a world where none may be perceived

Urban Legends have no real origins or their origins are lost

Urban Legends are memes

Part Two

Classic Urban Legends

A credulous mind finds most delight in believing strange things, and the stranger they are the easier they pass with him; but never regards those that are plain and feasible, for every man can believe such...

Samuel Butler, *Characters*

Classic Urban Legends

In this section some of the more famous and celebrated Urban Legends will be examined in detail. In addition, so too will some recent Urban Legends that have grown up around the attack and the destruction of the Twin Towers in New York in order to show how an event such as that one provoked a new series of tales to begin – some of which were reported in the global media as being true. With the Twin Towers we once again enter the realm of the Conspiracy Theory as a number of stories actually read less like Urban Legends and more like apparent factual events surrounding 11 September 2001.

The *'Teens In Peril'* Theme

Teenagers are one of the most important 'channels' for
the distribution of Urban Legends. This, in part, is due
to the fact that they span the two worlds of childhood
and adulthood. They are leaving one for the other and
therefore show subconscious fears about the world
around them. Psychologically the telling of the stories
expresses a desire to warn each other about the perils
they are about to face in the wider world. Teens tend to
be the most gregarious of all social groups, congre-
gating in clubs, pubs, colleges, universities and so on.
Other than in the media, these are the sites where the
transmission of Urban Legends is most widespread.

'The Boyfriend's Death'

The folklorist David R Barnes collected the earliest
known instance of this story in 1964 from a freshman
at the University of Kansas. Of course, that is not to say
that the story did not exist before. There are modern
twentieth century elements in it – the car, for example
– but the basic spine of the story may go back a long
time. The central motif is the 'couple' engaged in
behaviour that has always been frowned on. The teens

are transgressing social boundaries and must be 'punished'.

The most fundamental and unchanging elements of this story – the spine – are the couple in the car, the abandoned girl, the scratching noise, the shadowy figure, the daylight rescue and the horrible climax. Variations occur whenever and wherever the story is told but, as in Urban Legends in general, the core story remains the same. These variations are the regional location, the reason for abandonment, the rescuers, the details of the murder and the explanation provided for the place name.

This happened not long ago on the road that turns off Highway 'x' by the drive–in cinema. This couple were parked under a tree on this road and, well, it got to be time for the girl to go back to her dorm so she tells her boyfriend that it was probably time that they were going. But the car wouldn't start so he told her to stay in the car and lock the doors while he went off to the cinema to get help. Well, he didn't come back and then soon the girl started to hear scratching noises on the roof of the car. The noises continued and she got more and more scared. The boyfriend didn't return. Finally, when daylight came, some people came by and helped her out of the car and when she looked up she saw the body of her boyfriend hanging from a tree and it was his feet that were scratching against the roof of the car. That's why that road is called 'Hangman's Road'.

In some variations, to add an extra frisson, the girl is told not to look up by the people who rescue her. But she does so, with the inevitable consequences for her sanity. In this version of the story, notice that the rescuers are described only as 'some people'. As the story develops 'some people' become 'policemen'. Later versions even give the policemen lines to say. Usually they are the ones who tell the girl not to look up. Authority figures also lend credence to the story and add a greater sense of reality to the tale. Further developmental elements include the fact that the police are called by the missing teenagers' parents or are out on patrol when they come across a seemingly abandoned car.

'The Hook'

One source for *The Boyfriend's Death* Legend is *The Hook*, another classic example of the *Teens in Peril* theme that was first reported in the 1950s. Once more we find teenagers on a date in an isolated area in a potentially dangerous situation because they are acting just outside the boundaries of accepted behaviour. *The Hook*, however, is subtler in its subtextual warning not to misbehave since both protagonists escape with their lives.

A young man and his date pull into their favourite 'lover's lane' to listen to the radio and to make out. A warning on the radio that an escaped killer is on the loose interrupts the music. He is described as having a hook in place of his right hand. The couple become frightened and drive off. The young man takes his date home and goes round to open the door for her and discovers that a hook is caught around the door handle.

It is quite easy to see how *The Hook* soon developed into *The Boyfriend's Death* since they have much in common. By the time the latter tale appeared in the 1960s *The Hook* was already a favourite Urban Legend and it only took a degree of elaboration for it to evolve into the more sophisticated story.

Once more *The Hook's* killer changes from area to area. In one place he is a crazed lunatic who has escaped from an asylum. In another he is a convict. In some versions the couple begin arguing because the young man's advances become too amorous or the girl becomes scared by the radio report and demands to be returned home. The young man starts the engine and roars off. When he gets her home he goes round to open her door only to find a bloodied hook attached to the door handle.

In a sense *The Hook* is a perfectly tidy story with one plot point following on from the other but on the other hand (no pun intended) why would a convicted criminal be fitted with a hook? Why would this character appear just as his escape is announced on the radio? Why would the couple drive off just as the villain put his hook into the door handle? Would he not use his good hand to open the door? The more one analyses it, the more the story begins to fall to pieces.

Yet the elements in the story as it is told are open to all kinds of interpretation. The fact the young man revs the engine and races away out of annoyance reminds us of the original sexual purpose for the couple's presence in that remote spot. In some versions both the girl and the boy are sexually aroused. In other versions it is the young man's desire that is highlighted. Folklore specialist Linda Dégh also suggests that this story illustrates 'the natural dread of the handicapped'. Folklorist Alan Dundes disagrees, emphasising the curtailed sex quest in the plot. He adopts a Freudian approach seeing the hook as a phallic symbol that penetrates the girl's door handle, a hook that is torn off in an act of 'castration' when the car drives off at the girl's insistence. We may also see that the role of the radio is as the 'voice' of conscience – society's voice as it were, acting as a warning to the girl and one that is often (but not always, depending on the version) an irritation to the young man.

'The Baby Sitter and the Killer Upstairs'

This Legend is another classic of the *Teens In Peril* theme. A variation of it even appears as the opening scene in the film *Scream*. In this tale an unknown assailant who taunts her via the telephone harasses a lone female babysitter. It is similar to the *Killer In The Back Seat* (see below) and is in all likelihood a later variation.

There is a young female babysitter looking after two children, both in bed asleep, in a big house. She is

watching television when all of a sudden the telephone rings. Picking it up she hears this male voice
at the other end laughing hysterically. She asks him
what he wants but he will not answer. She hangs up.
Fretting for a moment she soon forgets the call and
turns her attention back to the television. Not long
after the phone rings again and she picks it up only
to hear the same maniacal laughing. She hangs up
again but, feeling really worried, she calls the operator who tells her to calm down and, if he calls again,
to keep him on the line for as long as possible so that
the call can be traced.

Not long after the phone rings again and, on
hearing the laughing again, she asks why the man is
doing this but he continues to laugh and ignores her
question. This time he hangs up and not long after
the operator calls and tells the babysitter to get out
of the house immediately. She does so but on the
way out sees a man, laughing hysterically coming
down the stairs covered in blood and carrying a large
butcher's knife. She runs out into the street just as the
police turn up, called by the operator, and they
discover that the man has killed the two children.

The set elements of this Legend are the late hour, a
female babysitter watching television, a mysterious and
threatening man who calls three times, an operator, a
call to get out of the house immediately and the frightening notion of the killer being in the house all the
time. The variations occur in the location (as always),
the number of children in the house, what the

murderous caller says to the babysitter (sometimes nothing more than manic laughing or simple threats) what the operator says to the babysitter ('get out of the house', 'don't look back', 'don't go upstairs') and the arrival of the police (sometimes the babysitter calls them, sometimes the operator). More often than not there are variations in the fate of the children the babysitter was looking after. They are always dead but sometimes they have been 'chopped to pieces', other times 'torn to bits'. One of the reasons for the power of this Urban Legend is that babysitting is such a common occurrence, such a normal, everyday activity and this grounds the story in reality despite the ludicrousness and illogicality of other elements – e.g. the technical difficulties of calling the main telephone from an upstairs extension are ignored. Of course nowadays the story will have adapted itself to suit the advances in telephony – including dialler display, number recall etc. These developments will not hinder the story's retelling. As we have seen before it will evolve and adapt to the modern world.

Sue Samuelson, another folklorist claims the subtext of this Legend embodies the idea of 'the reinforcement of the power of a patriarchal society' and the belief that a woman, in this case the babysitter (a kind of proto-mother figure), should follow the traditional values of homemaker and housewife and not distract herself with her own interests. The warning is evident in the fact that the babysitter is watching television while the children upstairs are being killed. In numerous Urban Legends, it is interesting to note that it is always the female protagonist who is in peril and that she is often the focus for the sub-textual warnings that breaking social norms will result in terrible consequences. Samuelson may be correct in her theory that the stories in *Teens in Peril* are biased in favour of a patriarchal view of society and towards a particular male view of women and their social roles.

The 'Road Legends' Theme

With the prolific use of the car it is no surprise that Urban Legends have grown up around their use. Stories such as *The Phantom Hitchhiker*, in all likelihood, existed well before the combustion engine and were doubtless known to stagecoach travellers prior to the twentieth century. The majority, however, do not appear to predate the use of the car.

'Killer in the Back Seat'

In many respects this tale is related to *The Babysitter and the Killer Upstairs*, and more often than not it is placed within the *Teens In Peril* category, but it is more accurately regarded as a *Road Legend*. It includes the woman (sometimes a teenage driver) in peril and the unseen killer but it takes place on the open road and has third act variants occurring in petrol stations or lay–bys. There is also a 'joke' variation of this story in which a man is apparently pursued across town only for the pursuer to hand over something of value to the paranoid recipient – usually a walking stick or umbrella.

A woman has been visiting friends and, on leaving their house, notices that, as she starts her car up, a suspicious vehicle behind her starts up its engine at the same time. It is early in the morning and there are no other cars on the road. She sets off and makes her way to the main road only to notice that the suspicious car is following her. As she continues on her journey the pursuer often brings the car level with hers but never overtakes. The woman is now really scared. She is so scared that she begins ignoring red traffic lights. Eventually she gets home and the car behind pulls into the drive behind her. Terrified the woman leans on the car horn and her husband comes running out and asks what the hell is going on. The woman tells him that the man in the car is following her so the husband grabs this man and threatens him. The man tells the husband that he saw a man's head bobbing up and down in the back seat of the woman's car and was trying to warn her. Opening the back door of the woman's car the husband finds a man hiding on the back seat.

One variation has the pursuing car flashing its head-lights to try and attract the woman or as an attempt to stop the killer in the back seat from actually attacking her. The character trying to attract the woman's attention changes from region to region and from decade to decade. In some stories he is a burly truck driver or rough-looking man – which adds weight to the perceived threat. Occasionally, and more controversially, the man is said to be black. Once more we can see that the subtext reflects social attitudes (often middle class) and, in this case, reveals an inherent antipathy towards people seen as lower class or from ethnic minorities.

Sometimes the finale of the story takes place at a petrol station where the attendant spots something amiss and tries to alert the lone woman driver by some extraordinary ruse. In one version the attendant informs the woman that the money she has used to pay for the petrol is fake and this allows him to lead her safely away from the car. Sometimes it is a man filling up his car who spots something in the back seat and guides the driver away. In yet another version, as the woman speeds along the road, the man in the pursuing car winds down his window and demands that the woman follow his exact moves. She does so and, by imitating the erratic driving of the car in front, manages to dislodge the assailant, armed with an axe or other lethal weapon, from the roof of the car. And finally another variation of this story takes place in a car park in which the tools of the killer are found on the back seat after a woman returns from a shopping expedition.

'The Phantom Hitchhiker'

The Phantom Hitchhiker (or *The Vanishing Hitchhiker*) is perhaps the most famous Urban Legend of all time and is one that is often told as a simple ghost story or as a 'legitimate' haunting. It is an Urban Legend, perhaps the only one that has made the transfer to the realm of pure ghost story. The story dates back, at least, to the 1930s but may be older. The basic idea of the 'ghost that disappears' predates the era of the automobile but, with the widespread use of the car, the story has spread to the point where occurrences are reported worldwide. The origins of these stories lie in the tales of the *Ghost Rider*, in which a young woman jumps onto a horse being ridden past a 'haunted' location. She then disappears when the male rider reaches his destination. These *Ghost Rider* tales are predominantly from the late 19th century and may reflect male fears of losing ground to newly empowered women. But one could also argue that it reflects male sexual fantasies born of a repressive and religiously moral era that felt under threat from new ideas like Darwinism. Either way it is a dominantly male sub-text that reveals itself.

There is even an older Chinese version in which the ghost of a beautiful young woman walks behind a man as he travels along a road until disappearing outside her parent's house further up the road. Her father then tells the young man that she has been dead sometime. It is important to note here that she walks behind him just as the young woman hitchhiker often sits in the back seat of the car. Another version of *The Phantom Hitchhiker* appears in the Bible, Acts 8: 26-39. The Apostle Philip baptizes an Ethiopian who picks him up in a chariot then promptly disappears. In Russia in the late 19th century one version of the legend dealt only with the 'third act', restricting the 'hitchhiker' element to a passing mention in the dialogue. A priest arrives at a house to offer the sacraments to a sick man only to discover that the woman who sent him there is, in fact, dead. The man, perfectly fit, who tells him this, her son, is promptly stricken with terror and dies that evening. The priest has to offer the sacrament.

There are numerous versions of *The Phantom Hitchhiker*. It is the Urban Legend that has more variations than any other, taking in ghosts, prophecy and even (in a 1960s version) Jesus Christ who, as a mysterious stranger, is apparently thumbing for a lift in some remote backwater. These tales seem to tap into the idea of lost souls wandering the world, people who have met untimely deaths either on the road or in war (sometimes the Hitchhiker is a soldier returning from war).

A man is driving along a country road on his way home when he stops to pick up a hitchhiker. The hitchhiker tells the man that he lives in a house a few miles up the road. They set off. The hitchhiker remains silent for the entire journey. When the man reaches the house he turns to tell the hitchhiker that they have arrived only to discover that his passenger has mysteriously disappeared. Puzzled the man decides to go to the house and tell the occupants what happened. On hearing of the man's description of his wayward passenger the people in the house tell him that the hitchhiker was their son but he's been dead for years and that the man is not the first person to have a similar experience.

In most reports, however, the hitchhiker is a young woman who chooses to sit in the back seat of the car and so can 'disappear' without the driver noticing.

Sometimes there is a driver and a passenger, which forces the young woman to sit in the back seat. In numerous versions of the tale the phantom hitchhiker leaves behind some physical proof of his or her presence – for example, a book. One object of 'proof' in a 1940s variation of the tale is an overcoat. When the hitchhiker, again a young woman, tells her driver that she is cold he offers her his overcoat, which she gratefully accepts. As they pass a cemetery she asks that they stop for a moment or two. They do. She gets out and wanders into the darkness. The driver and his companion (another variation) wait but soon their patience runs out and they go to look for her only to find the overcoat draped over a head stone – the name of which matches the name given earlier by the young female hitchhiker.

A variation of this Legend has prophetic words spoken by the mysterious passenger usually connected to a future disaster. This variation has its sources in ancient history since prophecy is an inherent part of many ancient tales. Sometimes the driver is a salesman; other times he is a cab driver. Sometimes it is a couple, and the male driver plays the dominant role in asking questions and engaging the hitchhiker in conversation. And the hitchhikers themselves range from quiet young women who are at best taciturn, to more talkative men who predict something miraculous. In one tale (from 1942) a couple give a ride to a lonely man who then tells them the war will end in July and that this prediction will come true as sure as they will have a dead man in the car before they reach home. The character disappears but further up the road an ambulance coming the other way crashes in a ditch. The driver of the ambulance asks the couple to take the patient to the nearest hospital but the patient dies in the car on the way.

'The Death Car'

As already mentioned, the proliferation of the automobile has brought numerous Urban Legends about its use and ownership. The *Death Car* is one that is not as famous as *The Phantom Hitchhiker* but, for a while, it was almost as common. It has a tendency to disappear for long periods of time then resurface for short periods only.

> A friend of a friend picked up this magnificent Aston Martin for only £500. The reason for it being so cheap was that it had been found in a field not far from the M25 with a body in the driver's seat. No one can get rid of the smell of death in it and that's why it's so cheap.

Once again the basic tale remains the same but the type of car, value and its location vary. Sometimes the corpse in the driver's seat is a suicide, in other accounts a murder victim. In some versions there is an awful bloodstain that, despite vigorous attempts at removal, remains stubbornly on view. In a number of versions the car is brought from a less than reputable garage and has to be returned, only for it to be resold to another customer who also complains about the smell and who likewise returns it.

With this tale, it is difficult to pin down a sub-text other than, perhaps, one of contamination by coming into contact with something so hideous. Some people have a fascination with collecting items that have a gruesome history. There is also the appeal of acquiring something so cheaply – always a popular motivation – but the added message is that one cannot realistically expect to have something so cheap without a sting in the tail or strings attached. The story embodies the idea of *caveat emptor* and there may not be a deeper meaning.

A more obvious meaning can be gleaned from a related car Legend *The Philanderer's Porsche* (or other expensive brand) in which the underlying idea is one of simple revenge and gaining advantage from another's misfortune – real *schadenfreude*. An advertisement is seen in a newspaper for a £50 Porsche. The interested party travels to the house (note that there are no enormous queues) and enquires about the price. They are shown the magnificent vehicle by a woman and the deal is made. The new owner asks the old why it is being sold so cheaply and is told that the woman's husband ran off with his secretary (lover, mistress etc) and told her to sell the car (sometimes the house, as well, and other expensive possessions) and send him the money. Warning bells ring immediately about the veracity of this story. Would it not be more likely that the philandering husband would head off in his Porsche? Would he really expect his abandoned wife to sell the house and sell it fairly? Would she really send him the money? Would she not, in reality, sell the car for a higher price and simply keep the money herself? As before, we see the problems of logic that arise when any Urban Legend is studied more closely.

The warning in this story is against infidelity in marriage and what to expect should one stray from the path. Once more, we can detect a warning to the male to beware of women or, alternatively, we can view this as nothing more than a good old-fashioned tale of revenge – a theme as old as humanity. In fact one could argue that the only person with any control in the story is the wife. Real control over the marital possessions rests with her.

The 'Nudity' Theme

Some Urban Legends are not full of murderous figures, gruesome discoveries or contamination and owe more to the notion of farce or comedy through the public exposure of the protagonist's naked body. This is a fear that we have all experienced at some time and one that is often expressed in vivid dreams as a universal embarrassment of terrifying 'exposure', of revealing ourselves to others. Our guard is down and we are therefore vulnerable. We are shown as we really are and not how we would like others to see us. We are literally 'stripped bare'. Many of these nudity-based Urban Legends have been rehashed in movies, TV sitcoms and adverts.

There are two famous nudity-based Urban Legends. The first is *The Stranded Man* and the second is *The Nude Surprise Party*.

A bachelor living in a high rise block of flats is running a bath and has therefore stripped. He hears the newspaper delivered (or letters) and, once he has stepped out into the hallway to collect it, the door slams shut behind him. It is, of course, now locked leaving him stranded.

This story appeared in the Russian novel *The Twelve Chairs* by Ilya Ilf and Yevgenii Petrov and in the Mel Brooks film of the same name, which may have added to its 'authenticity' and indeed its propagation. A US version of this story has a woman as its protagonist about to do her laundry. (Notice that it is a woman in a domestic situation again.) This Urban Legend has the feel of a joke.

> A housewife decides to do her laundry and goes down to the basement with its leaking pipes where she fills up the washing machine and decides to add the dress she is wearing to the wash. She spots her son's football helmet and places it on her head. So there she is stark naked except for the football helmet when she hears a cough. She turns around and finds herself staring into the face of the plumber. As he heads for the door his only comment is 'I hope your team wins, lady…'

Why, we must ask, would she feel better placing an American Football helmet on her head and not covering herself in a dressing gown? And would she not know that a plumber was in the house? And so on. Once more we see how certain aspects of the story start to break down under careful scrutiny.

In *The Nude Surprise Party* nakedness is not revealed to only one person. The protagonist is usually exposed to a large group of people, and, to make matters worse, the group is made up of friends and family members. The tales vary in length but usually have a basic plot line.

A businessman, feeling downhearted because everyone seems to have forgotten his birthday, is invited out for a drink by his understanding secretary. She takes him to an out of town place for lunch and a few drinks. On the way back to town the secretary invites the man back to her place for another drink. The man agrees. When they arrive the woman fixes him the promised drink then tells him she is going to slip into something more comfortable. Not long after she reappears with a birthday cake, the man's wife and kids and business colleagues to discover the man dressed only in his socks — having misinterpreted the situation.

In most cases it is the 'secretary' who takes on the role of pseudo-temptress who pulls the man into the embarrassing situation but, as Professor William Hugh Jansen of the University of Kentucky argues, this is a reflection of the male mindset. The man has 'underestimated his wife's memory, overestimated his secretary's pliability and overestimated his own sex appeal'. This is also evident in another version of the Legend.

A new member of staff, a young man, has come to work at an office. His secretary is an attractive young woman who is single. He asks her out on numerous occasions and she refuses every time. Until finally she invites the young man to her apartment for dinner. All through the meal she hints at a surprise for him. She excuses herself telling him she is going to prepare his surprise. Mistaking her intentions for ones of a sexual nature the young man undresses. Through the door to the bedroom he hears her ask if he is ready. He confirms he is. She flings open the door revealing the entire office staff gathered there to celebrate his birthday.

A version of this was used recently as the basis of an advert on UK TV for a particular brand of medicine.

One variation of the surprise story – a kind of bridge story between *The Stranded Man* and *The Nude Surprise Party* - is a tale about a babysitting couple who are cavorting around in the nude when the telephone rings. On the other end is the mother (of either the girl or the boy in whose house the story is set) who asks them to go down to the basement to turn off some domestic appliance – usually a washing machine. Both naked they descend the stairs (often in a piggyback) only to make the shocking discovery that both their families are downstairs throwing a surprise party. Sometimes a priest is in the family group to emphasise the warning about morality and the lack of sexual restraint exercised by the young couple. Some have suggested that going down to the basement can be interpreted as a Freudian symbol. In most versions of the tale the young girl is the one who ends up having the nervous breakdown, spending the next few years in an institution while, more often than not, the boy leaves town and is never seen or heard from again. A clash of generations can also be read into this tale or a telling account of the conflicts that arise between traditional values and those of a presumed 'immoral' younger generation. In every incident of this Urban Legend it is the morality of the older generation that triumphs which is odd when one considers that the story is nearly always told by the younger generation.

One subtype of the *Nudity* Urban Legend is the *Mistaken Identity Nude*. Oddly enough these tales often have a man of the cloth involved. In the classic of its type a man brings his minister/priest/rabbi/vicar home for dinner after helping him do some heavy duty manual work at the Church/Temple. The man invites the minister to use the shower upstairs. The wife hearing her husband come home but unaware of what has transpired hears the shower in use and goes into the bathroom. Feeling amorous she reaches around the shower curtain and grasp's the bather's penis. Pulling on it a few times she says 'Ding dong, dinner bell!' or something obscene and lascivious. Exiting the bathroom she discovers her husband coming up the stairs. This is similar to the more famous story of the woman coming home to see what she thinks is her husband working under the car. Reaching down she unzips his flies and pulls on the man's penis. Giggling to herself she goes into the house only to discover her husband sitting in a chair and reading the newspaper.

The 'Corpse' Theme

Death is often a taboo subject especially in Western cultures where it becomes something to push aside and ignore. When it does happen the death process is handed over to someone else to deal with (doctor, nurse, coroner, mortician). The fear of death is as great as ever despite medical advances and an improving life expectancy. Urban Legends have sprung into life to reflect our fear of the death process and this is best expressed in *The Runaway Grandmother*. These are often jokingly referred to as *dead loss* stories.

A family, mother, father, two children and grandmother are holidaying abroad. At some point in the journey one of the children says that grandmother won't wake up. Discovering that she has died the family decide to wrap her in a sleeping bag and secure her to the top of the car, planning to report her death as soon as they enter the next town. When they eventually reach the next town they immediately go to the police but on returning outside they discover that the car has been stolen and grandmother along with it. The car is never found.

Versions of this story are reported from all over the world. Some date back to World War 2 in which people fleeing occupied territories have to wrap a dead relative in a blanket but have the corpse stolen at a railway station. However, the tales' origins go back as far as the 18th and 19th centuries when they adopt the point of view of the thieves who, thinking they have purloined some valuable possession, are shocked to discover that they have stolen a corpse.

One important element is the lack of emotion that the family seem to have towards their dead relative. The corpse is always put on the roof almost immediately and without great debate – as if they are afraid of their proximity to death. There is always mention of the fact that the family now have more room, that a burden has been shifted away from them. And in all cases no one seems to be that put out by the fact that the car and their other possessions have been stolen – a price paid perhaps, for being rid of grandmother. The sub-text here is one of rejection of old age. In a youth-orientated society age is something to be shunned and old people are seen as worthless, offering nothing to society as a whole. The anonymous thief perhaps represents the third party who deals with the bodies of the deceased – morticians etc. The family do not have to bother even addressing the responsibilities of the grandmother's funeral or death process – someone has done that for them. Alan Dundes also interprets these details as a critique of Americans' principal interest in their relatives as nothing more than a source for money through an inheritance. In a very literal sense, they are disposable.

Some tales have a more developed third act in which the relatives, eager to get the body home, send it back but it goes missing en route. Or, more gruesomely, the body is cremated and returned as ashes to some relations. When the family return the relations thank them for sending them such 'wonderful curry powder' or 'such magnificent spice'. This element is known from a tale from the Renaissance in which a man sends his dead, dismembered friend home in a variety of pickling jars. On the ship home the various jars are stolen and their contents eaten.

This has direct links to *The Dead Cat in the Package* or *Cat Parcel* in which a newly deceased pet has to be disposed of. Various forms exist but the basic tale is straightforward.

An individual, often a spinster or a lonely woman, has a pet cat she dotes on. When the poor creature dies she decides that it has to be buried out of town because local law prohibits the disposing of animal remains in the street. The cat is wrapped in a wrapping paper or a box. On her way out of town the woman stops in a department store to do some shopping only to have the package stolen by a shoplifter. With her problem solved, although not in the way she planned, she decides to go home. On leaving the shop she discovers a crowd of people. Pushing her way through she sees a large woman collapsed on the floor – the package has split open and the body of the cat is visible.

As before, various odd actions reveal the story to be nothing more than an Urban Legend. Should not a town or city have a process for the disposal of dead animals? Why is the woman who has collapsed always overweight? Once more a woman is being punished, in this case for 'shoplifting'.

Numerous versions also have the package substituted for a 'prize'. In most cases, this is a large chunk of meat, usually ham. In one version of the story a man travelling to work offers to throw the body of the family cat over the side of the ferry but fails to do so. After accidentally leaving it in the parcel rack he nips back and grabs the parcel only to later discover, as he is about to tip the unfortunate creature into the bay, that there is a joint of meat in the package.

Sometimes the act of stealing the package is more obvious and the thief gets his or her just deserts almost instantly. The universal sub-text of all these kinds of stories – that 'stealing is wrong' – is made immediately apparent. 'Look what happens to thieves' is the clear message the narratives provide. Although the main players in this type of Legend tend to be women, the stories carry little or no overt and obvious sexist sentiment.

A more 'comical' version of the Legend has a family returning from a picnic with a selection of wild mushrooms or toadstools. Uncertain as to whether or not these things are poisonous they feed one or two to the cat. Nothing happens to the cat so the family cook the remainder and feast on them. At some point one of the family members looks out of the window and sees the cat dead on the driveway. They all rush to the hospital to have their stomachs pumped and return later exhausted and feeling sorry for themselves, only to discover that the milkman had accidentally run over the animal some hours earlier. A similar story line, one may remember, made up an episode of Fawlty Towers.

Some Other Famous Legends

Microwave Pet/Baby

Teens In Peril Subtype.

This one is often categorised under the *Teens In Peril* theme but has a wider context than that since its principal protagonists are not always teenagers. Like *The Phantom Hitchhiker* it is one of the most famous and celebrated Urban Legends and has, because of its simple premise, been reported all over the world.

> An old lady who has been given a microwave as a present by family members places her freshly bathed and still wet pet poodle in the oven to dry the creature off. After several minutes she opens the door to discover, of course, that the poor creature has been cooked to death.

Prior to the use of microwaves, the stories involved animals crawling into gas ovens or washing machines where they would meet a desperate end at the hands of an unsuspecting user of that device – either an old woman or a helpful young boy. Even as the microwave has become the favoured appliance in the stories, the two types of protagonist have remained the same. There are also stories of certain individuals attempting to dry their hair using a microwave and who suffer the fatal consequences of their actions or others working too near the open door of a microwave oven. (These versions ignore the inconvenient fact that the machines do not operate unless the door is closed.) All this represents an irrational fear of modern technology and a general ignorance of what 'microwaves' can do – evidenced in the lurid tales of exploding pets or eyeballs.

The other celebrated version is *The Wayward Babysitter* who, usually stoned on alcohol or marijuana (in the 1960s the babysitter, a hippie, was always high on LSD) ends up 'cooking' the child she is looking after. Once more note that the 'offending' character is female.

A couple hire a babysitter to look after their infant son and go out to a dinner party. Half way through the evening the mother calls home to see if everything is alright and the babysitter tells her that she has stuffed the turkey and put it in the oven. The mother does not remember having a turkey so she assumes something is wrong and the couple head home to discover that the babysitter has cooked their baby.

Some versions have the parents getting home just in the nick of time to save their infant and the only variation in the drug theme is one story in which the babysitter is driven out of her mind by the simple fact that the baby will not stop crying however much she tries to calm the child.

A celebrated variation of the *Pet In The Microwave* is the *Poodle In The Restaurant* in which a couple go into an eating establishment (usually in a foreign country to facilitate the misunderstanding) and order a meal. One of the couple points to the dog and then to their own mouth by way of indicating that the dog should have something to eat as well. The waiter obliges and takes the dog to the kitchen. Some half an hour later the waiter returns with a platter on which rests the poodle, now cooked, much to the horror of the couple. A fear of foreigners and their ways is being expressed here. The story is usually located in the East – particularly Korea where stereotypical views about that nation's cuisine allow the tale to gain credibility. There is an African version of this tale in which a mistranslation of a phrase that could either be 'sit the baby up' or 'cook the baby' results in the not too surprising conclusion.

There is a blending here of modern concerns (about technology) with more ancient fears (of child abandonment and infant death). With *The Wayward Babysitter* society's abhorrence of drugs manifests itself. The warning is that drugs are dangerous – not to the user but to those around them, in other words to 'normal', hardworking middle class people. This has echoes in modern Legends, frequently reported in tabloid newspapers, about people 'high on cannabis' running amok with guns and swords.

Douglas.

Alligators in the Sewers

Contamination

The Legend about alligators breeding in the sewers of New York has been around since at least the 1960s. Thomas Pynchon makes a reference to it in his 1963 novel *V*. The Legend still circulates today.

> Visitors to Florida brought baby alligators back to New York as pets, then, discovering that they were difficult to look after or simply tiring of them, they flushed the creatures down the toilet. The alligators took up residence deep beneath the streets, feeding off the rats, and have bred to the point that it is now lethal to venture into the sewers of New York City.

Stories of beasts lurking where they should not be have been around from time immemorial and reflect primitive fears about the world and about the 'darkness beyond the cave'. Humans are under threat from nature but not 'out there' – now the menace is directly beneath. In the aftermath of the events of the 11 September 2001 alligators in New York sewers may once more grow to prominence as fear of terrorism continues to rise – a fear of the threat within as opposed to the threat without.

With this tale variations tend to be minimal. One simple change that has occurred is that the alligators themselves have become albino or blind. In evolutionary terms this would take a long time and rests on a misunderstanding of how long it takes creatures to adapt to the dark. Once more, as is so often the case with Urban Legends, logical flaws in the stories soon begin to show up. Could an animal from hotter climes survive in a dark, cold environment? Would a young alligator survive the trauma of being flushed into a grim habitat? Yet real new stories continue to be reported which appear to lend some support to those who believe in the Legends. *Time* magazine of 21 June 2004 carried an article about a crocodile which had been at large in the streets of Hong Kong. The Yeun Long crocodile had attracted great attention from tourists and the authorities in equal measure. It had evaded capture for some time before it was finally cornered.

Kentucky Fried Rat

Contamination

As our food processing becomes more technology-driven there is a tendency for us to grow concerned about the methods employed. There is a real sense that the mechanisation of modern food manufacture makes it more 'alien'. The rise of instant meals prepared by others is now the norm. Assembly-lines, drive–in fast food outlets, and ready meals transfer the whole process to unseen hands. This, in turn, fuels a certain level of paranoia. There have been many 'horror stories', high-lighted in documentaries on national television, to add weight to our suspicions that all is not well in the food industry.

The basic Legend follows these lines:

A couple stops at a fast food outlet and orders a fried chicken snack. The husband returns to the car. As they eat the meal the wife says, 'My chicken tastes funny', but she continues to eat. After she complains one more time the husband says, 'Let me see it'. Turning the courtesy light on he discovers that his wife has been eating not a chicken but a rat – neatly floured and deep fried. The woman goes into shock and is rushed to hospital.

Sometimes, at this point in the tale, lawyers from the fast food company turn up and offer the husband a large sum of money to keep quiet and hospital staff are threatened, while the woman remains on the critical list. In some variations she dies and the narrator ends the story with the cliff-hanger element that the husband is now taking the fast food company to court.

In some versions of the Legend reasons for the rat being there then follow. Sometimes it is because of fumigation – the fast food outlet is riddled with rodents and the only way to cure the problem is through mass extermination. The rat, succumbing to poison, drops from the machinery into the batter mix to be deep-fried and served. Other variations offer more sinister reasons. A disgruntled employee who may have been passed over for promotion or has a grudge against his boss brings in a rat he has found and drops the deceased animal into the mix. Teenage versions often have a young couple at home in a romantic situation making the gruesome discovery which is reminiscent of *The Boyfriend's Death* and *The Hook*.

Once more, as in so many of the Legends, it is the woman who makes the awful discovery. As Fine suggests, 'by neglecting her traditional role as food preparer, she helps to destroy the family by permitting the transfer of control from the home to amoral profit-making corporations... the rat is appropriate symbolic punishment'. Once more a patriarchal view of woman is revealed as the subtext of the Legend. To add weight to this argument one version has a lazy wife serving up fast food chicken, usually in dimly lit surroundings, in an attempt to pass it off as her own, only to end up eating a fried rat as a punishment for her underhand behaviour.

European versions of the story have different contaminants in the food. In the UK it tends to be 'alien' meat in the curry – usually dog. In other countries it may be a rat bone that has to be removed from the victim's throat. On this side of the Atlantic the stories usually reflect a mistrust of 'foreigners' – the restaurants are all small, privately owned businesses run by 'outsiders'. In the US the food contamination stories are based on fears of the 'mighty faceless impersonal corporations'. This may change in the next few years – fear of those 'impersonal corporations' will, in all likelihood, become a fear of the 'outsider'. *The Kentucky Fried Rat* and other *Food Contamination* stories may well adopt sinister undertones – for example, the perpetrators of the 'crimes' or 'food terrorism' will all be of Middle Eastern descent.

The Ghostly Airliner

The Ghostly Airliner is another Urban Legend that falls into the category of ghost story. In its telling it is clear that it is centred on people's fear of flying and a deep mistrust of machinery. It is also related to stories like *The Deep Fried Rat* because it reveals a suspicion of the mighty aircraft manufacturers into whose hands passengers places their lives every time they fly. As there are jokes about 'Friday Cars', vehicles hastily put together at the end of the week, could there be such a thing as a 'Friday Plane'? Although air travel remains the safest way to travel it is still a scary idea to fly five miles above the earth with someone else at the controls. Our lives really are in the hands of others. Can they do their job properly? Do they know what they are doing?

A jetliner had crashed somewhere (again the locations are numerous) killing a good number of people on board, including the pilots, but the plane itself was not destroyed. The airline decided to save money by rebuilding the plane (variations have spare parts being used in other aircraft) and not long after it was back in the air. Soon passengers started hearing strange noises including the voices of those who had died in the earlier crash. Before long people grew hesitant about flying on that particular plane and custom dropped away. The plane was eventually taken out of service and now lies rusting in a hangar somewhere.

Would an airline really rebuild an aircraft that had been in a crash and put it back into service? How would other passengers know that the 'voices they heard' were from the crash? To make the story a shade more believable some variations have parts of the downed aircraft acting as spares in other planes in the fleet. A door handle here, a seat there and particular bolt somewhere else. It may appear to be more believable that an airline would save money by using the crashed aeroplane for spares but, of course, they would not. Accident investigators and the FAA or the CAA would see to that. In yet another version of the story the ghost of the Captain warns a stewardess that certain components in the plane are faulty and, sure enough, when the plane touches down (just) the warnings are found to be true.

The spare parts motif is one that appears in a number of other Urban Legends – famously in the ones that built up around James Dean's Porsche after his fatal crash. The story goes that a number of parts were plundered from the wreckage and used elsewhere in other vehicles. All the cars that had the spare parts installed into them also crashed and ended up either killing or maiming their owners.

Accidentally Funny

Another more precise form of Urban Legend is the funny accident, a story form that has developed and grown in recent years particularly through the Internet where it often appears as Xerox or Internet Lore. They are humorous stories but, unlike jokes, they do not have a punch line. They are just funny incidents. Examples of this include the story of the man who broke one or more limbs after throwing a rope over his house and tying it to his car bumper so that he could be hoisted up to fix a TV aerial or a leaking roof, only to have his wife drive off in the car. (Note that it is once again the woman at fault.) This may be a funny story but, under closer scrutiny, it appears totally ridiculous. Why not use a ladder? These stories always involve an individual engaging in ridiculous behaviour and are the Legends most likely to appear, unchecked, as tabloid news.

Other examples of this kind of narrative are the ones that appear in *Winnebago Lore*, a growing subset of stories that span neatly the themes of *Nudity* (for some stories) and *Legends of the Road* and also include *Insurance Excuses* (the daft stories of people making ridiculous claims on their insurance). The most popular story recently concerns a man who puts his Winnebago on cruise control then goes into the back to make a drink and wonders why the vehicle crashes after failing to negotiate a corner 'on its own'.

The 'Twin Towers' Legends

This section includes some of the best-known Urban Legends that have sprung up around the attacks on the Twin Towers. In all of these examples we have a *fixed point*, a source for the stories – one that is very real to all of us, thus adding great weight to the credibility of stories connected to the tragedy. Emotional gravitas is assured because the world watched the events unfold on television. The Twin Towers attack undoubtedly happened so why doubt the stories attached to that monumental event?

Many questions have emerged from the tragedy and will continue to do so but this is unsurprising in any event on such a scale. There is always a vast amount of reputable post mortem analysis but this often becomes clouded by reckless reportage and jumping to misinformed conclusions. Simple human flaws in intelligence gathering can often be seen as the subversive work of grand conspirators when, in reality, nothing more than incompetence is to blame. Official denial (often an attempt to save face and hide the aforementioned incompetence) adds to the proliferation of Urban Legends and conspiracy theories. Some of these were reported as late as 5 June 2004 (in the *Daily Mail*) in an article about a controversial book entitled *The New Pearl*

Harbor by David Ray Griffin. Once more Urban Legend and conspiracy theory blend neatly together.

The Jewish Conspiracy

Legend: Jews were warned not to turn up for work that day. This was because Israel was behind the World Trade Centre attacks but made the world believe it was the work of Arab extremists. A story in an 'Israeli newspaper' reported that thousands of Jews had been killed in the attacks. When this story was subsequently retracted the following day this was widely interpreted in the Middle East as an inadvertent leak that Jews in the World Trade Centre had in fact received a warning and that none had actually been killed.

Reality: Osama bin Laden has claimed responsibility for the attacks through numerous media channels. No warning was actually given. There is no evidence of any involvement of anyone other than Bin Laden, al-Qaeda and possibly the groups associated with his network. Many Jews were among the murdered and no reference is given to the specific 'Israeli newspaper' mentioned. It must be pointed out that the likely instigators of this tale were non–Muslims.

Urban Legends about Jewish conspiracies have been around for centuries – the fake document known as *The Protocols of the Elders of Zion* is a notorious example – and have attached themselves to a number of areas of modern culture from the media and global banking to Communism and Holocaust denial.

Stranger's Warning!

Legend: A mysterious stranger alerts people to lurking dangers. Wild variations of this rumour exist, including warnings not to drink Coke, take a train at a certain time or enter New York City on a specific date. They are said to come from a stranger, always Muslim, in a supermarket or indeed other public places, and they are given to those who help him out when he is short of change or who return his dropped wallet. Variants of this story occurred in the UK where numerous people reported being approached by a man of Middle Eastern origin who told them not to go to a particular Tube station on the anniversary of the destruction of the Twin Towers. The location to be avoided varied in some versions – Canary Wharf, Paddington Station, Trafalgar Square and the Houses of Parliament are all mentioned in addition to Tube stations.

Reality: This is undoubtedly an Urban Legend but the rumour forced organisations as different as Coca-Cola and the West Midlands police to issue statements to allay people's fears. Yet there is an obvious question that undermines the reality of the story. What is the motivation is behind the mysterious stranger's actions? The sub-text behind the story is that it is possible, if you act as a good Samaritan, to escape a chance terrorist attack. It diffuses the fear of being killed in such an attack. It could be argued that it is a way for someone to feel emotionally part of this kind of tragedy, that it caters to a psychological need to become involved. Because attacks have happened around the world this Urban Legend has a frisson of reality to it and thus becomes more resistant to scepticism. It is also worth noting that Coca Cola again features in the story (www.snopes. com, the website that chronicles Urban Legends, has a whole subsection on *Coke Lore*).

Bin Laden in Utah/Arizona/Florida etc.

Legend: Osama bin Laden has been sighted in Utah (and other US States). Since the attacks, there have been dozens of reported sightings of bin Laden in Utah, centring on the Salt Lake City area. Local people have reported bin Laden shopping or dining at McDonald's. He has also been reported in numerous other places, most controversially in Florida, the state run by Governor Jeb Bush.

Reality: Bin Laden is, in all likelihood, alive and hiding on the borders of Afghanistan and Pakistan. Why should Osama Bin Laden wander around a country he despises eating food that is wholly unfitting for his faith? Bin Laden loathes everything for which the US stands, so why should he be there? In some ways this parallels the 'mysterious stranger' story in that a ' dangerous foreigner' is perceived to be 'invading' the sanctity and safety of home soil. It is *The Babysitter and the Killer in the House* Legend re–shaped in terms of global politics – something dangerous and murderous lurks in the homeland. Yet, in one of this story's sub-textual messages, American values are re-affirmed. Even though Bin Laden claims to despise the US he cannot get enough of it. Even a major terrorist thinks the country is great and wants to be there. The story acts, in short, as a confidence restorer.

Domain Names

Legend: Several Internet domain names related to the attack had been registered beforehand. Many news websites reported that at least 17 different domain names relating to the attacks were registered 15 months and more before the attacks of September 2001. Examples were *towerofhorror.com*, *worldtradetowerattack.com* and *worldtradetowerstrike.com*.

Reality: None of these domain names relate to the attacks on 11 September, and the Twin Towers had already been the subject of a terrorist attack in 1993 so some may relate to the earlier attack. What is true is that people rushed to register new domain names after the attacks of 11 September (e.g. NewYorkCarnage.com). 'Two/Twin Towers' could also be a reference to *The Lord of the Rings* – the second volume in Tolkien's trilogy is called *The Two Towers*. (The use of Tolkien's title by film–makers was, bizarrely, considered insensitive by some people.) Even if domain names had been registered before the attack, what purpose would that have served? A warning? Why warn anyone about the attacks? If Bin Laden wanted to create maximum devastation, why give the US authorities ample time to stop the attacks?

Bin Laden Owns Top Bank

Legend: Bin Laden, or the Bin Laden family owns one of the world's largest financial institutions, Citibank.

Reality: The rumour is thought to have started when it emerged that the Saudi prince Alwaleed bin Talal had a 4.8 per cent holding of Citibank's stock. Talal reportedly has no connections whatsoever with bin Laden or any other terrorist group. Bush family ties to the Bin Laden family however are said to exist which adds further fuel to the fire. Financial institutions colluding with the enemy is not a new phenomenon. Banks such as BIS, Chase, Barclay and Westminster were all doing business with the Nazis during the Second World War (see *Banking With Hitler*, Timewatch BBCTV). It is not a great leap to assume the same is still happening today.

Why did this Legend spring up? What is its subtext? It seems to be connected to the *Deep Fried Rat* story or to any number of Legends attached to Coca Cola. A great corporation is seen to have too much power. The story reflects a fear of faceless multinationals exploiting the general public. In this case a more specific target can be attached in the form of Bin Laden who acts as kind of 'devil in the works' – the faceless corporations carry the face of the enemy.

Self-inflicted Wounds

Legend: The attack on the Pentagon was staged by US Authorities. French author Thierry Meyssan, who advances the theory in his book *9/11: The Big Lie*, claims the attack on the Pentagon was the work of the US military. This theory is also promoted in *The New Pearl Harbor* by David Ray Griffin. The attack becomes a US version of the Reichstag Fire, staged by the Nazis in 1933 and blamed on communists. Griffin alleges that the story advanced by the US government is an impossibility – for example, he claims, the hole in the side of the building is too small and the wings of the crashed plane would have swept forward to create a greater impact site.

Reality: One of Meyssan's main arguments was that only the exterior of the building was damaged, yet CNN proved this to be wrong, with photographs and footage detailing internal damage. However, it is unlikely that this Legend will fizzle out and recent developments within the US intelligence world, such as the resignation of George Tenet, the head of the CIA, will add to speculation and help the story to endure. As with the controversy that surrounds Area 51, official denials boost the legitimacy of any Legend. Political resignations and firings suggest, to many people, a cover up.

Survivor Sex

Legend: Hospitals saw a sharp increase in births nine months after 11 September. Numerous newspapers, magazines and websites claimed that, in the aftermath of the Twin Towers attacks, hundreds of couples suddenly realised the value of life and decided to have a child - or just wanted more sex.

Reality: Hospitals in New York and across other states reported no great increase in births. Some hospitals reported fewer than normal. Did the Legend reflect a perceived threat to the existence of the US? A subconscious fear that citizens were about to be annihilated in the 'Armageddon'? To avoid being exterminated the obvious solution is procreation. Many US citizens, when interviewed in the streets at the time, thought that the end had indeed come and that the 'invader' had finally arrived. The stories of increased pregnancies and births act as reassurances that a way of life will continue and will not be swept away.

A Released Arab Convict Flew One of The Planes

Legend: A freed Arab terrorist was responsible for the Twin Tower attacks. Several media outlets reported that an Arab terrorist named Mahmoud Mohamed Atta, jailed for life for his part in an attack on a bus in Israel in 1986, had been released and was one of the pilots flying the planes on 11th September.

Reality: This is nothing more than mistaken identity. There was a Mahmoud Mohamed Atta convicted of terrorism, but he was not the same Mohamed Atta involved in the World Trade Centre attacks. The story probably reflects fear and suspicion of those in power –

that they are failing their citizens by releasing dark forces into society.

Betrayal Of The Victims

Legend: The victims' fund is being channelled to terrorists. Following the publication of an article in *The Wall Street Journal*, the National Legal and Policy Centre claimed a $170,000 grant meant for victims of 11 September was instead being used to provide legal protection for suspected Arab terrorists.

Reality: This is entirely false. The New York Legal Aid Society said the funds were being used for the victims of 11 September who needed legal advice. Once again faceless corporations are blamed for working with the enemy and as with the *Deep Fried Rat* or *Coke Lore* they are seen to be playing or gambling with our lives.

All these terrorist-based stories echo *The Killer Upstairs* Legends but on a national rather than personal level. Instead of a murderous madman upstairs we are faced with the 'evil foreigner' bent on the destruction of our way of life. The 'fear of foreigners' motif has been present in stories for a long time – it is best displayed in Urban Legends about 'The White Slave Trade', in which white Anglo-Saxon females are whisked away by nefarious dark-skinned 'foreigners' to a life of sexual enslavement. The same motif is also reflected in alien abduction scenarios. It would not be surprising if, after the attacks of the 11 September, 'abduction' tales, as well as those of contamination, increase in the telling and the reporting.

Part Three

The Future of Urban Legends

Trust a witness in all matters in which neither his self-interest, his passions, his prejudices, nor the love of the marvellous is strongly concerned. When they are involved require corroborative evidence in exact proportion to the contravention of probability by the thing testified.

Thomas Henry Huxley

Proliferation

It is easy to forget that Urban Legends are not confined to a twilight world where peculiar little tales are told in darkened dormitories about backwater roads in which hook–handed killers lurk. These stories are around us all the time and because we have become so used to them and they have become such an intrinsic part of our society we constantly allow them to slip by without a second thought. We laugh at situation comedies, for example, in which a character finds himself naked at a party, unaware that it is the retelling of an Urban Legend. We accept them too readily, perhaps, and thus they are able to proliferate so easily, in the memetic sense, throughout our culture. Urban Legends appear in television commercials, in newspapers and television news bulletins (without any questioning of their veracity), and in films. The Internet allows Urban Legends to spread instantly around the world and there are numerous websites dedicated to the study and collection of these stories as they appear.

In many ways Urban Legends have reached saturation point and there are far too many for even the most experienced folklorist to consider. Indeed, odd as it sounds, we have reached a point where many Urban Legends are faked. They have no track record, no thread of story telling, no inheritance, no moulding of their structure – they just arrive, fully formed,

*in the cultural realm. Yet, perhaps, in a world of instant grat-
ification, we need instant stories to thrill us and, although the
power of such stories is reduced, this represents the ultimate
fate of Urban Legends.*

The Internet and Urban Legends

The Internet fulfils some of our desires for instant gratification. We can access imagery, information and knowledge faster than we have ever done in the past. However, the Internet is not as interactive as we are led to believe. Human interaction is still vital – as it is for the transmission of stories. The Internet offers an ersatz community and one with only a digitised human face. Urban Legends need the human element – they need an emotional connection through which to survive. The storyteller adds emotional depth, adapts the material, and engages the audience in a dramatic journey. These do not exist on the Internet. A screen is no substitute for the faces of fellow human beings. At best the internet will be nothing more than a repository for these tales, where the facts of the story can be studied more carefully. But will this represent an end for Urban Legends? The simple answer is no. New developments have begun. *Internet Lore* has simply replaced *Xerox Lore*. Emails with 'true' stories or photographic attachments (*Photo-Legends*) have proliferated wildly.

The 'Photo-Legend' is a recent addition to the process by which Urban Legends are transmitted. This is an Urban Legend in the form of a photograph illustrating either a classic story or simply a unique and bizarre happening. Some of these Photo-Legends are blatant forgeries but some are more skilful and, because they are photographs, they are more easily believed. An instant image is far more evocative than words, particularly in a modern world which desires information instantaneously but there are dangers inherent in this.

The camera never lies, we are told, but, in fact, cameras do. Very often the images on display are questionable. Sophisticated computer software has made the notion of a truthful image an outdated one – if, indeed, it ever was a reliable idea. www.snopes.com offers not only a comprehensive collection of stories but also logs Photo-Legend images with a rating guide as to their veracity. It proves that, just as not everything we read is true, so not everything we see is fact.

In the newsletter of the International Society For Contemporary Legend Research No. 53 December 2002, a report on the 2001 ISCLR San Antonio meeting records Jan Brunvand's argument that, since the 1980s, the Urban Legend, 'has much less vitality as an oral narrative genre'. This was due, he said 'to the migration of contemporary legends from folklore to popular culture where they have become stereotyped, standardized, exploited, and repackaged in a number of ways', adding that 'the Internet and not oral tradition now serves as primary mode of transmission for contemporary legends and we can no longer "collect" them, in the conventional sense of the term'.

Some other folklorists are more brutal when it comes to the role of the Internet, condemning it outright for the death of the folk tale. Linda Dégh, in *Legend and Belief* (2001), dismissed on-line legend telling as 'an activity for the socially challenged', wondering whether 'chat-group members will eventually come to the point of leaving the safety of their homes and entering real relationships'. This is too harsh since the Internet is of enormous value, if only as a storehouse for Urban Legends. The Internet does not represent such a big obstacle to the telling of Legends as Dégh suggests nor does it lack the levels of critical deconstruction required for proper analysis of them. In a lot of respects it is a healthy environment for the propagation of the Urban Legend genre. The meme has adapted to new circumstances, nothing more.

Hollywood and Urban Legends

Film, television and the world of advertising have all plundered Urban Legends. This is not always due to a dearth of new ideas, but because the iconic events allow an instant access to the subconscious. These stories are instantly recognisable and thus more readily slip into our reckoning to make a lasting impression. By association we may link *Nude Surprise Party* with a brand of alcohol or a medicine (and indeed vice versa). The killer in the movie may hold a greater power because we are subconsciously aware of the motifs used within the film's screenplay. The horror genre is the one which has most frequently made use of Urban Legends and *The Hook*, *The Killer Upstairs* and *Teens In Peril* have all transferred neatly to the screen. The films of the 'stalk and slash' variety and the more potent 'killer on the loose' sub-genre owe their existence to classic Urban Legends and draw their deeper meanings from them. More often than not and, even though they are branded as mindless horror movies and are generally abhorrent to the political Right, these films contain moral messages and should not be readily dismissed. Because of their roots in Urban Legends they bring with them the sub-texts associated with the Legends.

The film *Ring* and its sequels actually pretend to be Urban Legends, using a haunted videocassette as their mythological spine. Each film's story is presented in a faux Urban Legend style and pretends to be one that actually exists.

Even 'zombie' films carry a subtext that is recognisable from Urban Legends. The zombies represent unthinking, soulless outsiders – the 'alien foreigner' – and draw upon 'body contamination' motifs to add to their potency. In *28 Days Later*, the zombies multiply through a transmittable and highly contagious virus – a clear reference to *Body Contamination* Legends. Even when the overall meaning of a film is different, it often contains similar motifs to those found in Urban Legends.

Scream, Scream 2, I Know What You Did Last Summer, The Nightmare on Elm Street series, the *Halloween* movies and *Urban Legend* et al, all tap into Urban Legend elements such as hook-handed killers, lonely roads, imperilled babysitters, lone females and so on. The film *Candyman*, for example, has its killer sporting a lethal-looking hook while the female protagonist, played by Virginia Madsen, is researching Urban Legends. It is interesting to note that in film versions of Urban Legends the young woman is very often the one shown to be in control. The moral heart of the movie, unlike that of the source material, often resides in the female protagonist. This no doubt reflects the shifting position of women in society and may be one good reason why this genre of film is so reviled by the Right.

In *Nightmare on Elm Street* the legendary Freddy

Krueger and his 'bladed' fingers (for 'blades', read 'hook') is the equivalent of the killers found in the more gruesome Urban Legends. As Wes Craven, his creator, says, 'Freddie is an entity that has been around for a very long time. He stands for something ancient and probably goes back to the very roots of mankind. In each age storytellers try to grab on to those elements that are mysterious and hidden and ineffable and give them shape and give them names. In my case it was Freddy'.

These films are popular because they 'exploit' well-founded fears about the world beyond our comfortable boundaries. However, as in Urban Legends, we are not directly involved so there is the safety net of distance, which offers us catharsis and a release valve for our fears. The enduring popularity of films like *Psycho* and *The Texas Chain Saw Massacre* is based on the fact that we know the killers portrayed in light and dark on celluloid really do exist out there. Ed Gein (who actually used meat hooks), on whom *The Texas Chainsaw Massacre* and other films like the 1974 movie *Deranged* was loosely based, Harold Shipman, Charles Manson, John Wayne Gacy, Fred West were all actual people and the crimes they committed were horrific and very real.

Harold Schechter, Professor of English at Queens College New York, has said, 'What you see in that film (*Texas Chainsaw Massacre*) is really a version of a very old and widely distributed kind of folk story about taboo rooms or houses that you are forbidden from entering. But of course people do enter and what they discover there is a room full of dismembered corpses and they themselves are then killed and dismembered. So the facts of the Gein case became assimilated in this kind of story. It's as though there is some kind of archaic level of our minds that makes sense of these horrors in terms of these stories'. (Quoted in *Clive Barker's A-Z of Horror* – BBC Books)

Schechter also suggest that we should 'read *The Texas Chainsaw Massacre* as a fairy tale which has a great deal to do with the Vietnam War anxieties among the young. It seems to be a vision of America transformed into this vast killing machine that you know is feeding off its own young'. As we have seen, Urban Legends reflect the anxieties of the society in which they are set. When they are transferred to film the sub-texts of the Legend very often go with them.

There are of course numerous Urban Legends that attach themselves to films e.g. *Poltergeist* and the mysterious deaths of cast and crew related to the film, the ghost supposedly visible onscreen in *Three Men And A Baby*, or the Coen Brothers' *Fargo*, and its claims to be based on a true story. Although the Fargo screenplay is fiction, this has not stopped people from looking for the 'treasure'. A 'documentary' was even made about a girl looking for the money, who ended up meeting an untimely death, thus adding another level of credibility to the Legend. In reality the programme owed more to *The Blair Witch Project* than to a real incident. This is symptomatic of an increasing blurring of the boundaries between reality and myth and is a further example of the fact that we find it hard to distinguish between the two.

It is safe to conclude that, through the media, Urban Legends will continue to influence us. But could they be put to nefarious uses? Can they deceive us in more deliberate ways? Can Urban Legends be a useful tool for social control?

The Political Use of Urban Legends

Although many Urban Legends include racist and sexist stereotypes at their heart, these are not always obvious at first glance. Even if they are, we tend to accept them and move on to enjoy the story. *The Hook, The Babysitter and The Killer Upstairs, The Boyfriend's Death* and other Legends remain relatively innocent stories, albeit ones that carry a social warning. But could Urban Legends work as a powerful tool in politics? Should we be concerned about the patriarchal attitudes towards women that they sometimes express? The simple answer is yes – and sexism is not the only problem. Other Legends carry disturbing subliminal messages.

In recent years the fear of the 'alien foreigner' has grown stronger. This has found expression in the nonsensical idea that anyone of Arab origin has to be a terrorist or, at least, must be treated suspiciously. Innocent people are arrested 'just in case'. (One terrorist suspect, Abu Hamza, even has a hook for a hand – a useful and ironic gift to the Legend makers.) We only have to examine some of the Urban Legends that have their origin in the attacks on the Twin Towers to see what is happening. In numerous tales 'the white man' is the one under threat. These motifs are not discouraged because, in short, they are useful tools for social control. Legends that promote simplistic ideas of 'nationhood', ignoring all social and economic problems, are encouraged and people are duped into believing lies.

Not only do these stories encourage a subtle form of nationalism but they can be manipulated to ensure that a politician who can tap into the national psyche and the fears within it is guaranteed to be elected. In the same kind of way, fundamentalist religious organisations have played on people's fears by developing ridiculous stories about devil worship in remote communities. An Urban Legend about child molestation by Satanic groups was circulating in the 1980's in the US and, not long after, found its way to the UK. Here it was picked up and taken seriously by authorities who were duped by a myth. Subsequently perfectly innocent families suffered badly, particularly in the Orkney Islands where a community was torn apart by what was, in short, nonsense. The same thing happened in South Africa where rumours that Satanic cults were working to bring down society were encouraged by a fundamentalist Christian chief of police. Also from the wilder shores of Christianity we have Urban Legends about bodies being weighed on the point of death and dramatically losing 'x' amount of mass, which is instantly attributed to the 'soul leaving the body' – a deliberate fabrication designed to persuade a population to trust in the church and unquestioning faith.

Urban Legends about drugs also proliferate, designed

to encourage a simple-minded view of drug use. One Legend suggests that anyone using cannabis will be turned into a drug-crazed monster who will inevitably go on a rampage to rape and murder innocent woman and children. Such tales were first heard almost a hundred years ago and originated in the US where racist elements were added in which the drug-crazed killer was an African-American. Once more a fear of the outsider or dangerous foreigner was encouraged. One Urban Legend encouraged throughout the 1960s was that marijuana that had been flushed down the toilets was starting to grow in the sewers beneath New York (echoing similar stories about alligators in the sewers), thus enhancing the notion of drugs as 'excrement' on the level of 'the sewer'.

Urban Legends have even been used in psychological warfare. During the 1950s the CIA were involved in trying to suppress the Huk rebels in the Philippines. They researched a local Urban Legend about a creature called the 'Asuang', a vampire figure that stalked the Huk territory. CIA Pysch-war units would follow a Huk patrol and then ambush the last man who would be swiftly dispatched and left with two puncture marks in his neck. When his body was found by the rebels their fear of the creature and the Urban Legend would be enhanced and they would retreat out of the area.

On a more 'harmless' level the greatest Urban Legend of the 20th century was the idea of Flying Saucers and all its accompanying phenomena. The whole panoply of conjecture, psychology, misinformation, lies, bluffs and social tricks were a political invention to hide the damaging fact that the USA was using Nazi scientists, engineers and technology to gain ground against the Russians. Enemies had become friends and friends, enemies. For six years the Allies fought a war against Hitler. To begin working with Nazi Germany's greatest minds might have appeared a betrayal to those who had fought and died. So, a cover story was developed and allowed to grow, encouraged in the wings by the intelligence services. It succeeded beyond even their wildest dreams.

We are surrounded by powerful Urban Legends and to treat them as just harmless stories or to ignore them would be dangerous in the long run. Some, perhaps many, can certainly be dismissed as politically neutral but, in many others, there is a powerful sense that all is not well. Sexist and racist ideas lurk beneath the surface. There are also Urban Legends that are politically motivated and we should be aware of this when judging their credibility. As Douglas Rushkoff, Professor of Virtual Culture at NYU and Social Theorist, has said, 'Today, communication is the science of influence.' We should be wary of accepting what is written or published as the gospel truth and remain conscious that we may very well be falling under the spell of the 'science of influence'. We need look no further than the lies and half-truths about the reasons for going to war with Iraq for further evidence.

Urban Legends in the Making

Urban Legends about alien abduction have evolved over the decades from the simple meeting with denizens of another world to encounters with more sinister grey aliens who seem to be far more aggressive in their activities. This simply reflects the growing fears around the world of which this set of Urban Legends is symptomatic.

The Flying Saucer Urban Legend, as already mentioned, was one that was developed by the US military after WW2 to hide the fact that they were using Nazi scientists and Nazi technology. (It is often 'forgotten' that, without Nazi scientists, man would not have reached the moon.) The Nazis were developing saucer craft as weaponry delivery systems – the US and the Russians took this technology along with rockets and missiles and developed it. The best way to hide the testing of these craft was to spread rumours that they were from outer space. Any witnesses to the craft would be labelled crackpots and the notion of 'flying saucers' rejected as the work of fantasists. Even the top UFO investigation group was a product of the military. Everything was carefully stage-managed – even Hollywood helped spread the Urban Legends. Once the basic ideas were in the public domain the whole process accelerated. New developments included stories such as Roswell in which a flying saucer is said to have crashed (in reality, this is a merging of events which took place over a fifteen-year period and none of them has anything to do with alien bodies or captured disks) and the Bermuda Triangle, supposed site for mysterious disappearances of ships and aeroplanes (in fact, no more go missing there than in any other comparable region of the world). Flying Saucer 'thinking' has grown to take in New Age philosophy, (pseudo) archaeology and US military technology. It has acted as a springboard for a whole new wave of Urban Legends involving human hybridisation (these are all based on a complete misunderstanding and basic ignorance of the way genetics works), extraterrestrial colonisation, faces on Mars, government collusion with alien entities and the imminent arrival of 'Saviours' from outer space. The latter stories gain a further potency by blending in religion and become the source for a whole new gamut of ridiculous ideas.

In 'alien abduction' stories several different types of idea combine. The 'flying saucers' are apparently physical phenomena with a basis in reality (military hardware) whereas the 'abduction' part of the story is psychological and, in the fear of the 'foreigner' that it reflects, echoes a classic Urban Legend motif. Alien abductions differ from Urban Legends in that the abductee tells the story as a firsthand account – it did not happen to a friend of a friend. But, in many instances, abductees may be drawing upon the Urban

Legends, subconsciously picked up through the media, that have developed around extra-terrestrial life. Over the years the entities involved have varied so much that, if we believe all the stories, Earth must be being visited by thousands of different aliens which seems unlikely. The entities, like their technology, have changed over decades to mirror the changes in our world. Early flying saucers had 'valves', later ones had 'silicon chips' and, more recently still, the technology has often been subtly hidden, beyond the comprehension of the abductee involved. These changes are all a direct result of the progress of science. In many cases technology appears bizarre, almost mystical, to ordinary people. To paraphrase Arthur C. Clarke, any future technology will be indistinguishable from magic. In these stories, as in all Urban Legends, a deep-seated fear of some aspect of the world – technology, foreigners, contamination, failing morality and so on – is being expressed. In some cases the sinister 'greys', according to their abductees, are flying around in vehicles that are strewn with rubbish and highly unsanitary. The odd suggestion seems to be that, even though they can travel vast distances through space, they are incapable of cleaning up. The comments become less odd if we assume that they owe more to our own world than to any alien spaceships. We can indeed travel great distances and have made dramatic advances in understanding but we remain woefully reckless with our environment.

Another example of an emerging Urban Legend, one that has been recorded particularly in Africa (and also in parts of Russia), is the appalling idea that underage sex is a way to cure AIDS. E-petitions (another phenomenon of dubious legitimacy) have spread the rumours that men in South Africa are raping underage children as a way to cure the HIV virus and as a method of revenge. Undoubtedly rapes do occur but there is nothing in South African culture that even hints that sex with a virgin may be a curative procedure. This has more in common with long-discredited theories from the past such as the notion that the disease called the 'King's Evil' could be cured by the King's touch or the idea occasionally expressed in the Victorian era that sleeping with a virgin was a cure for various venereal diseases. (In reality, sleeping with a virgin simply meant one could not acquire a sexually transmitted disease but this obvious fact was given a more insidious interpretation.)

In certain communities in South Africa girls as young as 12 years old are often seen with older men and this is a mark of status. This perfectly ordinary cultural phenomenon, seen through the racially biased lens of western eyes, is open to misinterpretation and is the likely source for this Urban Legend. Misinformed Western media would do better to focus on real problems such as poverty, sanitation and the lack of any economic infrastructure which South Africa shares with so many countries in a similar socio-economic position rather than spread these kinds of stories.

It is clear that, at any given moment, there are always Urban Legends in the making. As soon as there is a new social development – in science, medicine or politics – stories about it, usually loaded with misconceptions and ignorance, spring up. Some start as rumours and continue as such until they fizzle out. Some, of course, go on to develop into fully fledged Legends. Predicting which ones will die out and which ones will survive as Urban Legends is usually very difficult.

Urban Legends: Good or Bad?

The most socially powerful Urban Legends carry a hidden moral message and many are also steeped in a patriarchal ideology which, consciously or subconsciously, is woven into the tales. Women are often perceived either as helpless victims or the wrongdoers in the stories. They are shown as weak links in society who have to be constantly reminded of their second class status. Yet Urban Legends remain convincing and continue to have a real power to dupe us. Even the classic stories, which have been around for a long time, still have a degree of 'what if' believability that continues to make them proof against critical assessment.

Urban Legends reveal the psyche of a nation and the best way of assessing them is to begin by asking what they tell us about a nation and how it feels about the world and its citizens. Outsiders, aliens and paranoia, for example, seem to have become an American preoccupation in recent years. Even relatively innocent Urban Legends that were once transported to America by Europeans are now changing and being re-transmitted to the rest of the world, loaded with these extra meanings. As the world changes, Urban Legends adjust to fit new world-views. However they now embody unhealthy ideas – distorted perspectives on other cultures, notions of national superiority, support for the suppression of women, young people, foreigners and others. If we continue to accept these stories we continue to accept prejudices and that is dangerous.

It is wrong to accept Urban Legends as simply trite but harmless stories. They are loaded with misconceptions and social deceptions. If we accept them without question then the memes that are Urban Legends and the potent sub-textual messages they carry will go on polluting our subconscious. We have to question their veracity and their meaning or we will continue to be 'programmed' by their hidden messages. Urban Legends need to be questioned in the same way as other cultural and social phenomena if we are to gain a healthy perspective on them..

Survivability

The human capacity for self-deception is evident throughout history. Even in the modern world, with all its discoveries and its greater understanding of the workings of the universe, superstitions still flourish. There are those who still salute magpies to ward off bad luck. Some people still think that breaking a mirror brings trouble or that images can be stored within them. We still talk of luck as a 'force', as something substantial that has direct influence on us, although modern science makes it clear that this is an illusion and that there is no force at work called luck. We assume that good and evil are real artefacts in the real world when they are, in fact, our own mental constructs. Some people, holding racist and ignorant ideas about ancient people, believe that they could not have built the pyramids and that therefore they must be the work of extra-terrestrials. Others believe a deity created the world in six days. (Why six days? If the deity is all-powerful, could it not have been done instantly?) If we can believe these fantastic notions, it is easy for other illogical ideas to spread like wildfire.

Not only in the peasant homes, but also in the city skyscrapers, there lives, alongside the twentieth century, the thirteenth. A hundred million people use electricity and still believe in the magic powers of signs and exorcisms… Movie stars go to mediums. Aviators who pilot miraculous mechanisms created by man's genius wear amulets on their sweaters. What inexhaustible reserves they possess of darkness, ignorance and savagery.

Those words are from Leon Trotsky and they describe Germany on the eve of Hitler's take-over. Is there much difference from the modern world? Will Urban Legends die out or are they with us for as long as we tell stories? Are they destined, inevitably, to fade away? There is no evidence for the inevitability of their decline. On the contrary, they may reach such a point of sophistication that they become indistinguishable from real history. In some instances, they have already done so. Urban Legends have a rich and fertile medium in which to grow – and that is human society with its readiness to accept the bizarre and reject the rational.

Behaving as the memes they are, Urban Legends are now adapting to new modes of transmission – most importantly, the Internet and the World Wide Web. There seems little doubt that Urban Legends will survive and thrive for as long as there are people to tell them and societies which allow the unquestioning faith required to believe in them.

Conclusion

At their most fundamental level, Urban Legends are simply tales of human beings in extraordinary situations which offer warnings about the terrifying world that exists beyond our most rose-tinted, comfortable and blinkered views of reality. They serve as reminders that all may not be well and caution us against complacency in morality and social mores.

They also indicate people's evolving concerns and fears over time. Some stories disappear for long periods when their underlying meaning becomes of no concern to the storytellers. At the same time old ones re-surface or new ones emerge and continue to express innate and very human concerns about the world at large, 'the dark beyond the cave'.

The stories often embody the clash between older and younger generations and, in them, the older social norms always win through. The younger transgressors are punished for their disrespect for society's rules. Urban Legends can be deeply racist and sexist. Foreigners from different ethnic groups are objects of suspicion. Women often figure in the stories as either perpetrators of crimes or victims who, through their social transgression, bring their own deserved fate upon themselves. Not all the victims in Urban Legends are female but, by and large, women suffer most in them. And too often the stories blame all of society's errors and failings on women, particularly if they also happen to be wayward teenagers.

Urban Legends are mirrors of a society. In them we see our obsessions with death, madness, psychotic killers and bodily contamination. Often Urban Legends can be difficult to separate from real history. They distort events and cloud the issues – the tales that have attached themselves to the Twin Towers bear witness to this. A tragic event is somehow demeaned by the proliferation of extraordinary stories, some of which verge on the comical.

Beneath their trite simplistic story lines Urban Legends carry a greater meaning. They cannot simply be dismissed as silly stories intended only to amuse and entertain. On the contrary they hold a great storehouse of information and misinformation. Understanding the meanings behind Urban Legends helps us to understand the psyche of a nation and, through them, we glimpse the prejudices and fears that exist within it.

The Should or Turn

Harley Davidson

Lucky images

Unlucky objects/things

Glossary of Terms Used
in the Study of Urban Legends

Visual legend object

Adaptability

How adaptable is an Urban Legend? One that can adapt easily to a variety of locations will survive longer than one that has a *fixed point*. The more elements within the story, the more adaptable it will be to a variety of geographical locations.

Conversational Genres

rumour

The distinct ways in which humans communicate (jokes, gossip, anecdotes, wisecracks, proverbs, nicknames, chitchat, conversations etc) and through which folklore is transmitted.

product myths

Communal Re-Creation

adverts
"buzz"

How the legend varies in the telling as it is passed from person to person. Each person will add their own elements and remove others, thus contributing variations to an overall story in which the core elements remain the same.

Communicative Event

Name given to any occasion, formal or informal, when social interaction allows the transmission of information. A business meeting would be an obvious example of a formal communicative event while a dinner party would be an informal one.

Fairy Tale

Predominantly European term for fictional folktales involving heroes and heroines, magic, faraway places, lost realms and imaginary peoples. Alien abduction and UFO urban legends owe much to this style of folklore (see *Passport to Magonia* by Jacques Vallee). Some folklorists use the term 'Wonder Tales' or the German expression *Marchen*.

Fallacies

These are minor legends that take the form of misconceptions about the world e.g. that hair and nails continue to grow after death, hair turns white overnight after a shock, a drowning person surfaces three times, eating fish is good for the brain and so on.

Fixed Point

Any location that is immutable in terms of the source of the Urban Legend. Urban Legends that spring up around the destruction of the Twin Towers will not transfer to any other building.

Folklore

These are the traditional story elements or beliefs in a culture that are told and retold, existing as oral traditions or customs.

Folktale

A generic term for fictional narratives in direct contrast to Myths and Legends, which are believed to be true or told as such. Folktales or folk narratives include tall tales, jokes and fairy tales

Informant

This is the storyteller – not so much the source of the story as the conduit through which the story passes. In Urban Legends the source is unknowable. Informants may be singers, craftsmen or folk healers – anybody who passes on information.

Joke

A funny tale with a punch line that falls into the category of folktale. Like Urban Legends there is often a moral element to a joke that may or may not be deeply hidden as a subtext. Some Urban Legends sound more akin to jokes than stories.

Legend

These are folk narratives that deal with realistic events that happened sometime 'in the past'. There is always the suggestion that Legends are true and that they are retellings of actual events. They often contain supernatural elements.

Levelling and Sharpening

Coined by University of Minnesota sociologist Gary Fine, this refers to the process by which only the gruesome aspects of an Urban Legend are remembered and retold, thus adding an overwrought, emotive response in the listener.

Motif

An element of a tale such as a character, object or action. Motifs are the elements around which the story is constructed e.g. haunted car, a maniac with a hook, a ghost, a body in a bed and so on.

Oral Literary Criticism

The process in which the storyteller attempts to explain the Urban Legend after recounting the tale.

Oral Tradition

The word of mouth transfer of stories, jokes, myths and

gossip – the verbal telling of tales. This term is sometimes used in reference to the customary transmission of behavioural and material folk traditions.

Ostension

Ostension is a folkloric term for the process of unwittingly acting out or mimicking the greater part (if not the entirety) of an urban legend that is already part of the body of folklore. If, for example, the events described in an urban legend, which had been around since the 1960s were played out, spontaneously, in real life in 2004, then that would be an example of Ostension. Pseudo-ostension is the act of deliberately acting out an existing urban legend (e.g. children secreting pins in their Halloween treats to throw a scare into the community or pranksters in Pulaski, Virginia, placing syringes in payphone coin return slots in 1999).

Photo-Legend

This takes the form of a photograph or series of photographs that illustrate some unusual event, usually something that is false. There is a propensity for Urban Legend Photographs to be fake, often appearing on the Internet. Occasionally Photo-Legends accompany newspaper articles.

Pivot Point

The point in any legend where the believable switches

into the unbelievable or where the normal becomes the abnormal e.g. the killer in a *Teens In Peril* legend sports an unusual murder weapon like a metal hook. The killer element is 'normal' but the fact that he sports a bill-hook, a glove of needles or a scythe tips the story into the abnormal.

Proto-Legend

Usually a folk belief or rumour that may very well develop into an urban legend.

Relative Chain

The chain along which the story has apparently trav-elled. e.g. 'I heard this from my mother's hairdresser's cousin . . .' or 'A friend of a friend of a friend told me that….' The permutations of the Relative Chain are almost limitless.

Rumour

An anonymous and unverified story that has a short lifespan which may very well, under certain circum-stances, develop into or contribute to the growth and spread of a wider Urban Legend.

Subtype Or Subset

A group of Urban Legends that branch off from a main story type but share many of the same story elements.

Theme

The general topic of an Urban Legend such as *Body Contamination* or *Death Car*. It can also refer to the viewpoint or underlying message that the tale carries.

Variant

A term for any text of an Urban Legend or a distinct and well-developed group of texts.

Xerox Lore/Internet Lore

Urban Legends that are circulated in and around offices as photocopied sheets of paper. 'Xerox Lore' has now given way to 'Internet Lore' where e-mails of stories are sent to other computers within a company or externally.

Some Further Reading and References

Websites

www.snopes.com
www.urbanlegends.com
www.mystical-www.com

Books

Alexander, Marc, *A Companion To The Folklore, Myths and Customs of Britain*, Bath: Sutton Publishing, 2002

Balkin, J.M., *Cultural Software*, Yale University Press, 1998

Bennett, G., *Traditions of Belief: Women, Folklore and the Supernatural Today*, London: Penguin Books, 1987

Blackmore, Dr Susan, *The Meme Machine*, Oxford University Press, 2000

Blum, S.H. and L.H., *Do's and Don'ts: An Informal Study of Some Prevailing Superstitions*, Psychological Reports 35: 567–571

Brunvand, Jan Harold, *The Vanishing Hitchhiker*, London: Picador, 1983

Brunvand, Jan Harold, *The Study of American Folklore*, New York: W.W.Norton and Co, 1980

Campbell, Joseph, *The Hero With A Thousand Faces*, New

York: Pantheon Books, 1949

Campbell, Joseph, *The Power of Myth*, New York: Doubleday, 1988

Dawkins, Richard, *The Devil's Chaplain*, London: Weidenfeld and Nicolson, 2003

Dawkins, Richard, *Unweaving The Rainbow*, London: Allen Lane/Penguin Press, 1998

Dawkins, Richard, *The Extended Phenotype*, Oxford: Oxford University Press, 1982

Dennett, Daniel, *Kinds of Minds*, London: Weidenfeld and Nicolson, 1996

Dennett, Daniel, *Darwin's Dangerous Idea: Evolution and The Meanings Of Life*, New York: Cornell University Press, 1998

Keary, A and E, *The Heroes of Asgard*, London: Macmillan, 1968

Kick, Russ, *You Are Being Lied To*, New York: The Disinformation Company, 2001

Kick, Russ, *Everything You Know Is Wrong*, New York: The Disinformation Company, 2002

Lynch, A, *Thought Contagion: How Belief Spreads Through Society*, New York: Basic Books, 1996

Randi, James, *Film Flam! The Truth About Unicorns, Parapyschology and Other Delusions*, Buffalo N.Y.: Prometheus Books, 1982

The Reader's Digest, *Strange Stories, Amazing Facts*, London, The Reader's Digest Association Ltd, 1975

Sagan, Carl, *The Demon Haunted World*, London: Headline, 1997

Shermer, Michael, *Why People Believe Weird Things*, New York: Henry Holt and Company/Owl Books, 2002

Spence, Lewis, *Introduction to Mythology*, London: Senate, 1994

Thompson, Stith, *The Motif Index of Folk Literature*, Bloomington: Indiana University Press, 6 Volumes, 1932

Vallee, Jacques, *Passport to Magonia*, Chicago: Henry Regnery, 1969

Magazines

The Fortean Times
The Skeptical Inquirer
Foaftale News: The Newsletter of the International Society for Contemporary Legend Research (Recommended)

If you have enjoyed this book you might enjoy these other forth-coming titles from the same series

1 903047 44 7
SCIENCE FICTION FILMS John Costello £4.99

1 904048 39 0
JOEL AND ETHAN COEN Cheshire & Ashbrook £4.99

1 904048 36 6
QUENTIN TARANTINO D K Holm £4.99

1 904048 33 1
THE CATHARS Sean Martin £9.99 (hardback)

1 904048 37 4
THE OSCARS John Atkinson £4.99

1 904048 34 X
THE HOLY GRAIL Giles Morgan £9.99 (hardback)

1 903047 97 8
BRUCE SPRINGSTEEN Peter Basham £4.99

1 904048 38 2
THE CRUSADES Michael Paine £9.99 (hardback)

1 904048 35 8
URBAN LEGENDS Nick Harding £4.99

1 904048 30 7
BOHEMIAN LONDON Travis Elborough £9.99 (hardback)

1 904048 40 4
SCOTT FITZGERALD Richard Shephard £4.99

1 903047 50 1
NAZI WAR TRIALS Andy Walker £9.99 (hardback)

Or browse all our titles at www.pocketessentials.com

Available from all good bookshops or send a cheque to: **Pocket Essentials** (Dept SS), P.O. Box 394, Harpenden, Herts, AL5 1XJ. Please make cheques payable to **'Oldcastle Books'**, add 50p for postage and packing for each book in the UK and £1 elsewhere.

US customers can send $8.95 plus $1.95 postage and packing for each book payable to; **Trafalgar Square Publishing**, PO Box 257, Howe Hill, North Pomfret, Vermont 05053, USA email tsquare@sover.net

Customers worldwide can order online at www.pocketessentials.com